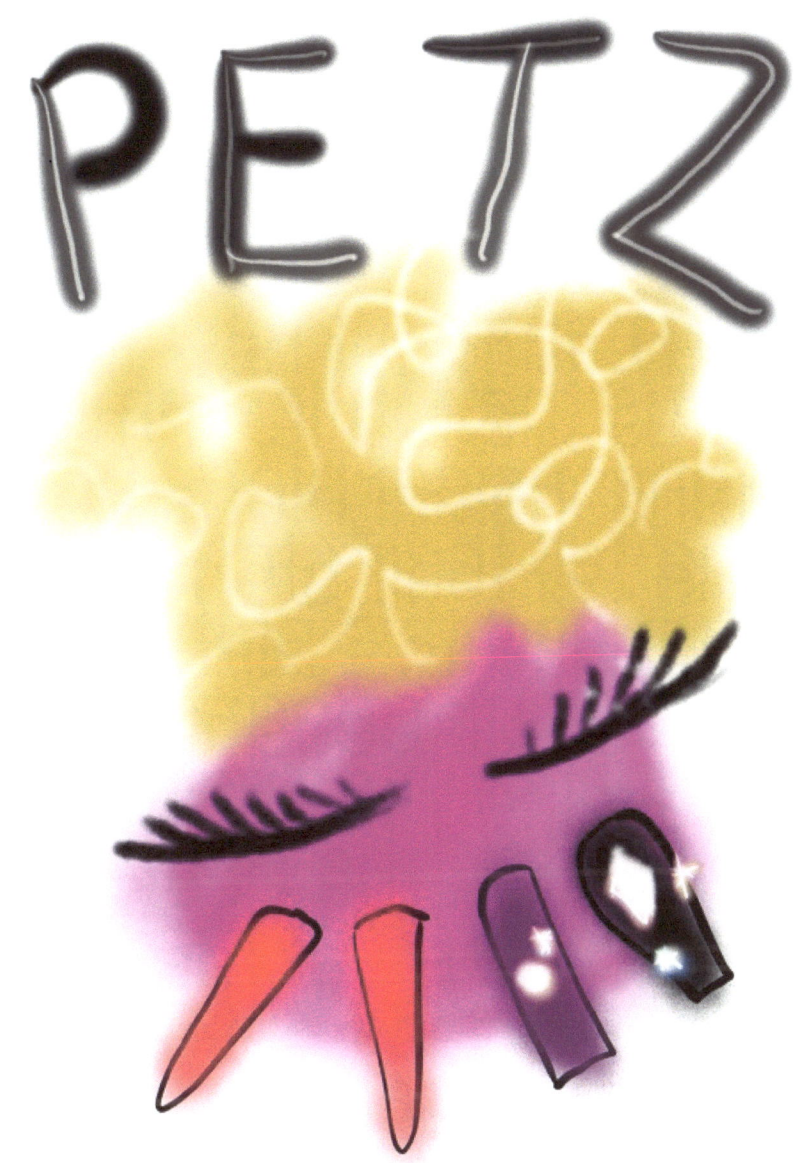

PETZ

Petz
♡ dreams com true ♡

- Made from recycled plastic
- Endless possibilities
- Share your creature on social media!

Hello and welcome to the world of Petz. A world where dreams and silliness come together. In this book, you can meet new friends made by us the Müller family. These nonsensical blobs become reality and tell their stories. They have never had this platform before but thank goodness we live in an increasingly inclusive world that has brought the Petz to us. Why not have a go at making your own Petz? It's easy because it can't ever be wrong. I'm sure you could come up with a great idea!

Silly petz

My Very Silly Petz, has ears that aren't a threat, just a squishy blob and a lovable petz.
What a Funny thing , with fur of Indigo, the neighbors all say, what the wackiest show.
Crazy for My Petz, I love to play and fuss, my bestest friend and one of us.
Silliest Petz in Town, jumps constantly and all around, one look and you know pet wears the crown.
It's Not Ordinary, It's My Silly Petz, I can't help but smile and I never forget.

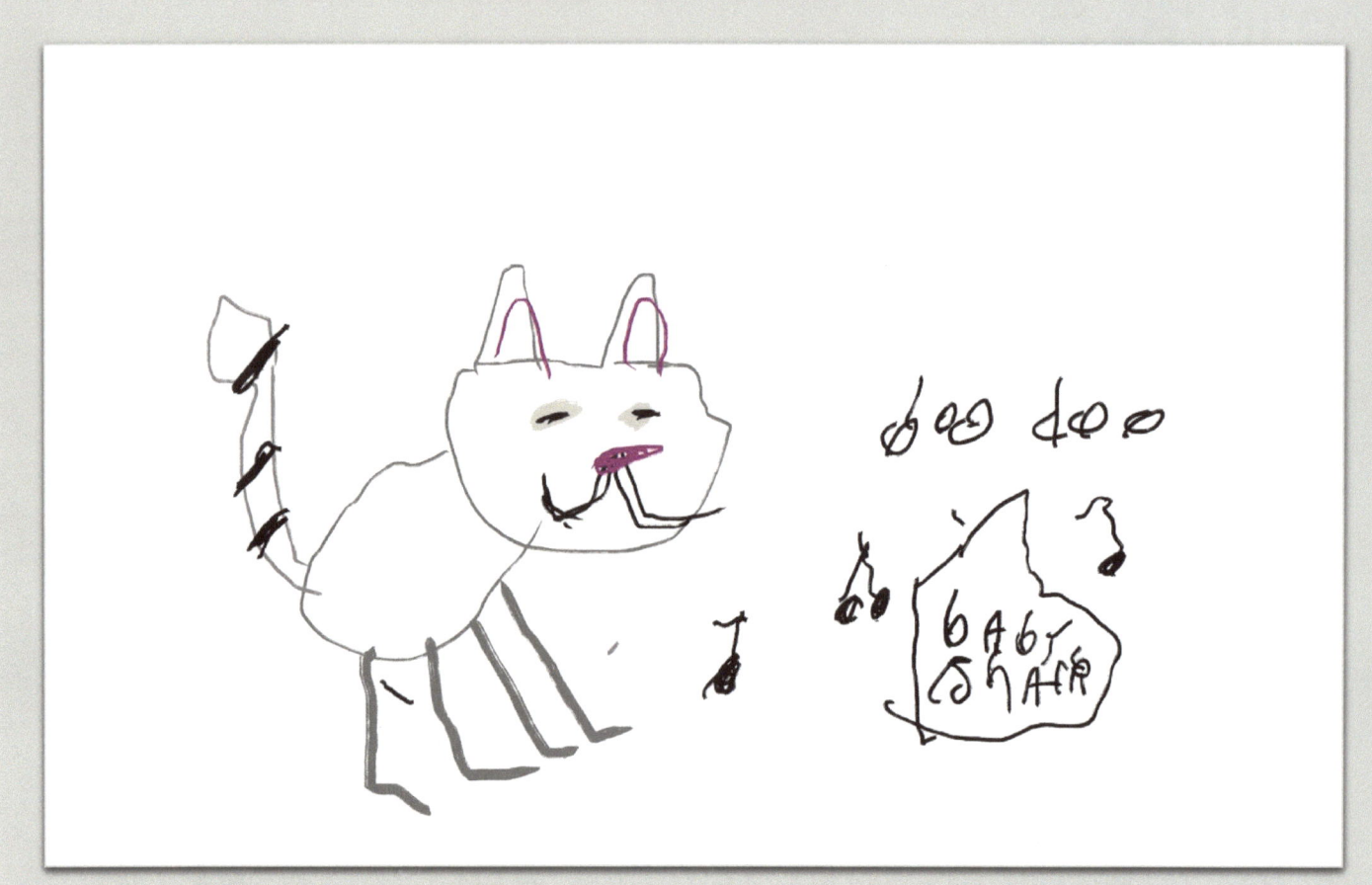

Kitti

This petz is very cute and is also symotanously highly annoying. They blast nursery rhymes antisocially through the night.

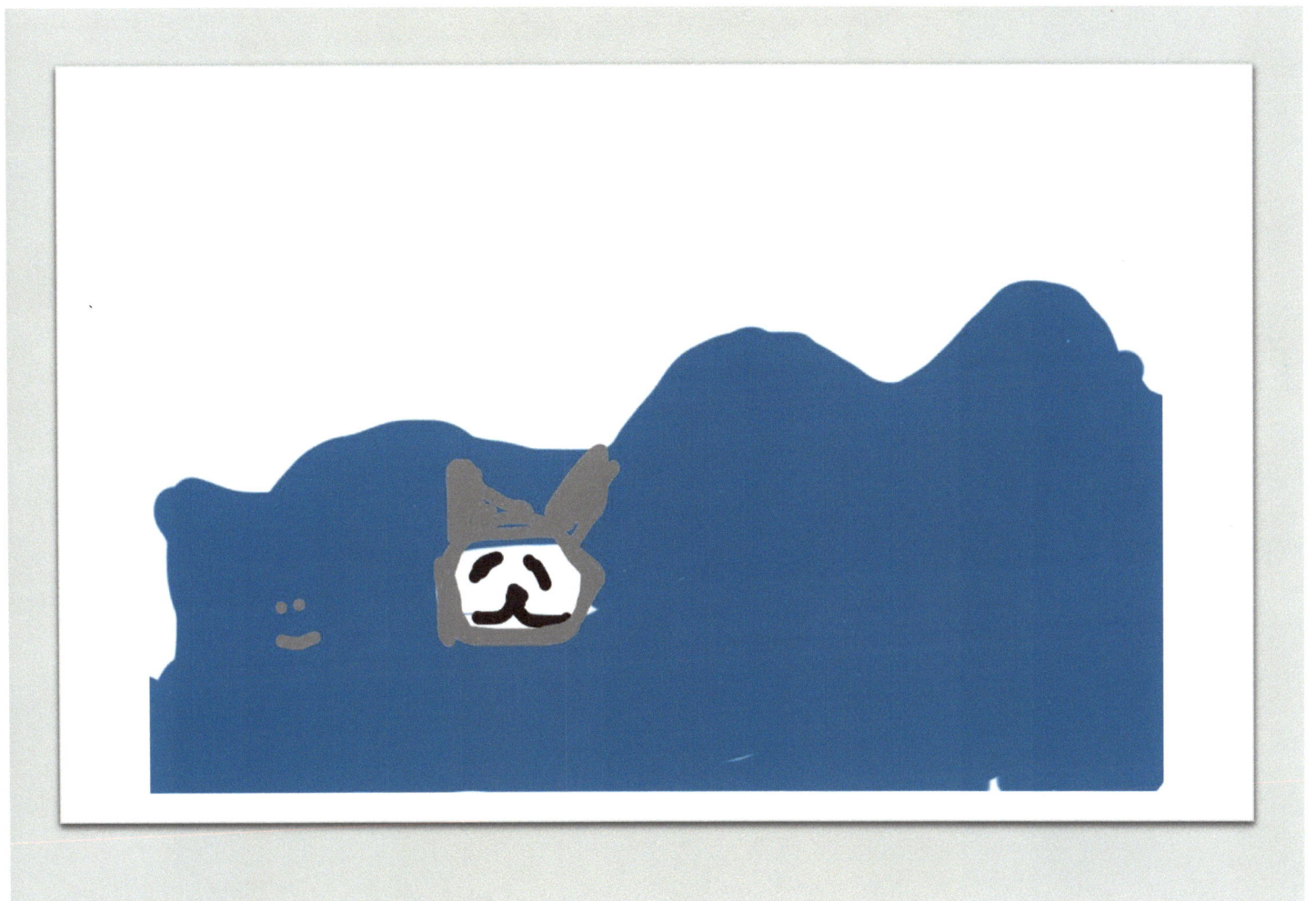

Zensiorkittizen

The evolved kitti. This petz can turn anything in to a complete disaster within seconds. Their super move is flooding bathrooms.

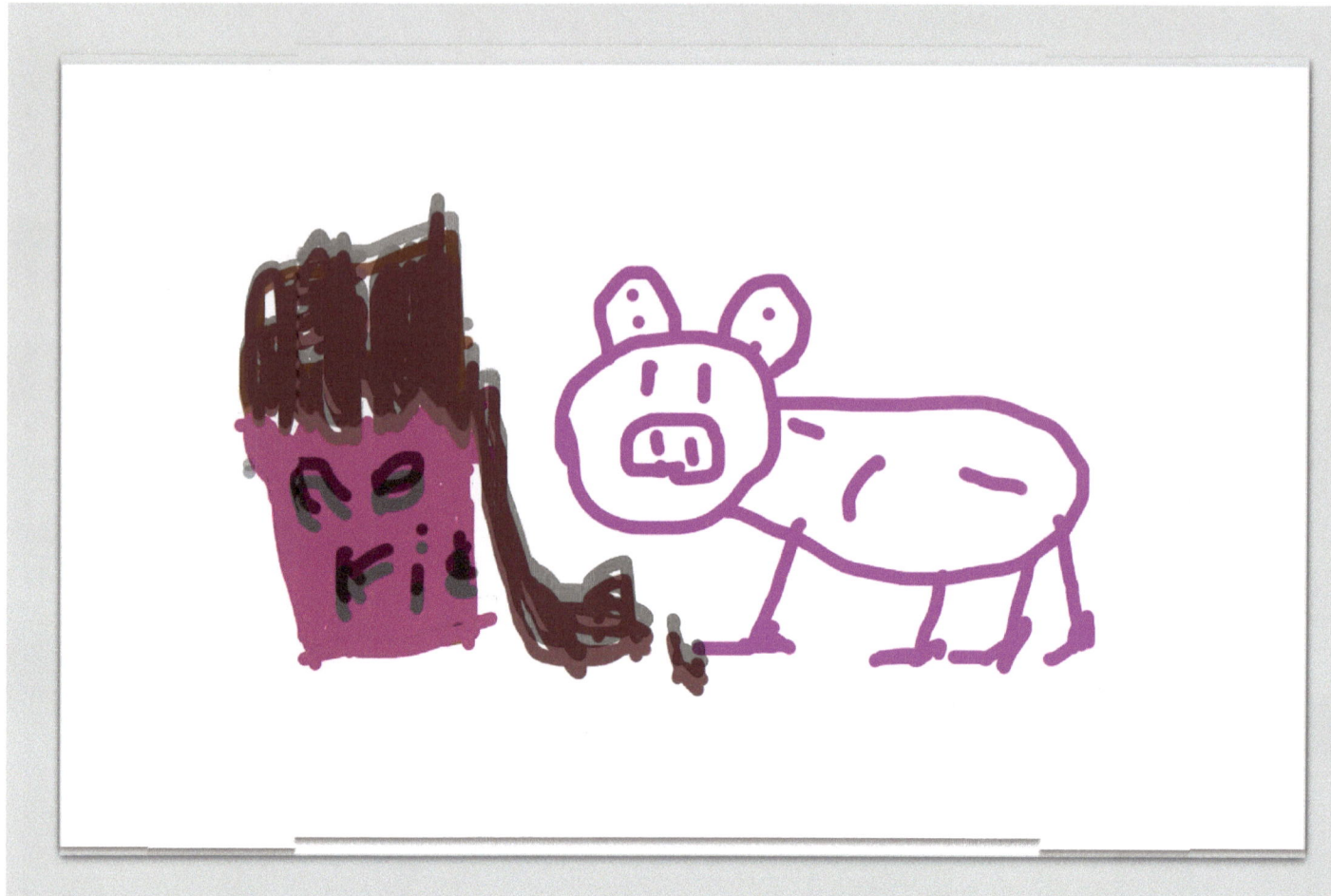

Piggyungry

They never stop eating snacks they can't eat a meal. even when they are eating snacks they are crying and sniffing out more snacks. They are never satisfied.

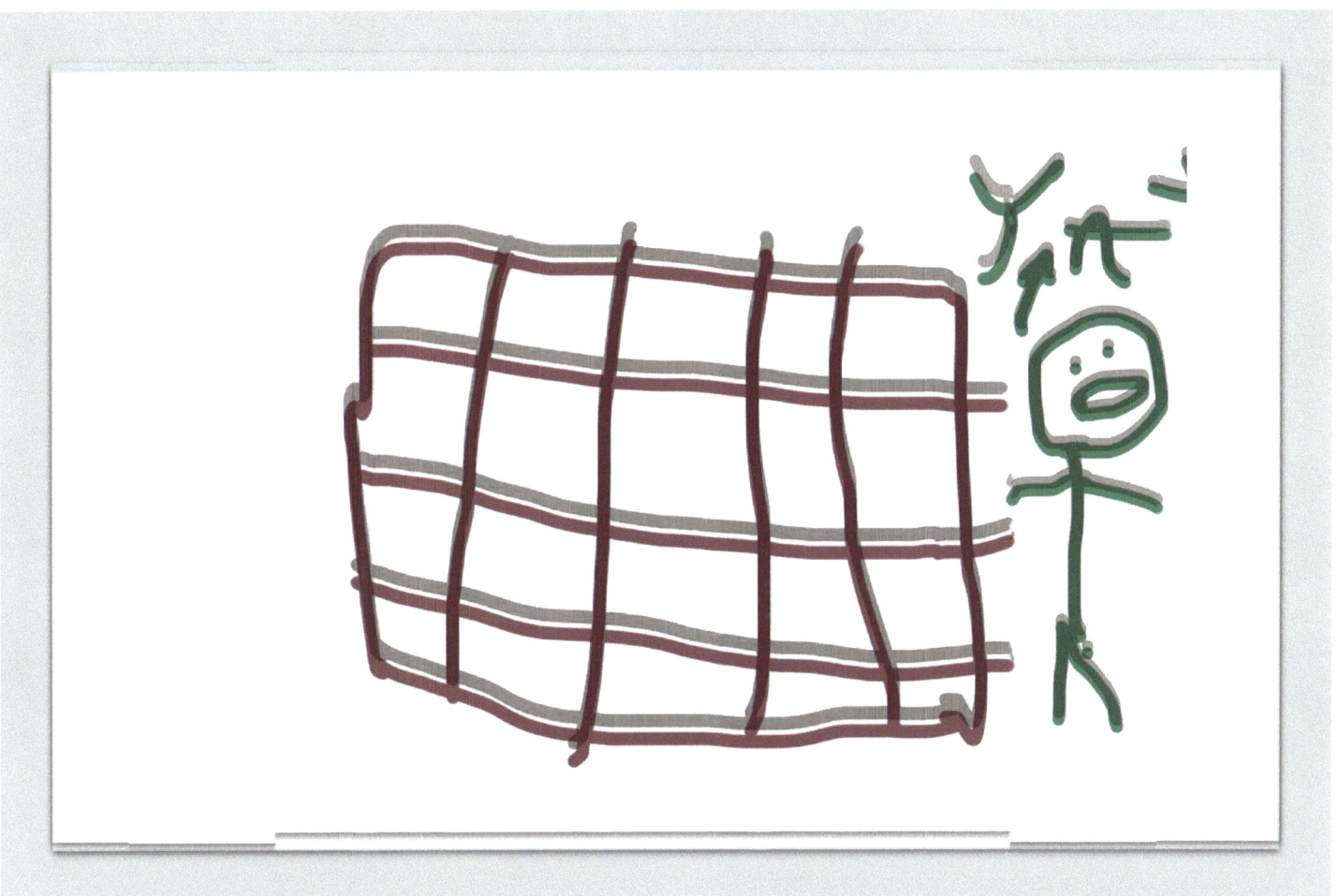

Kengle

Now this Petz is insane he only eats chocolate, He only drinks chocolate and If you turn him inside out he looks like a chocolate bar.

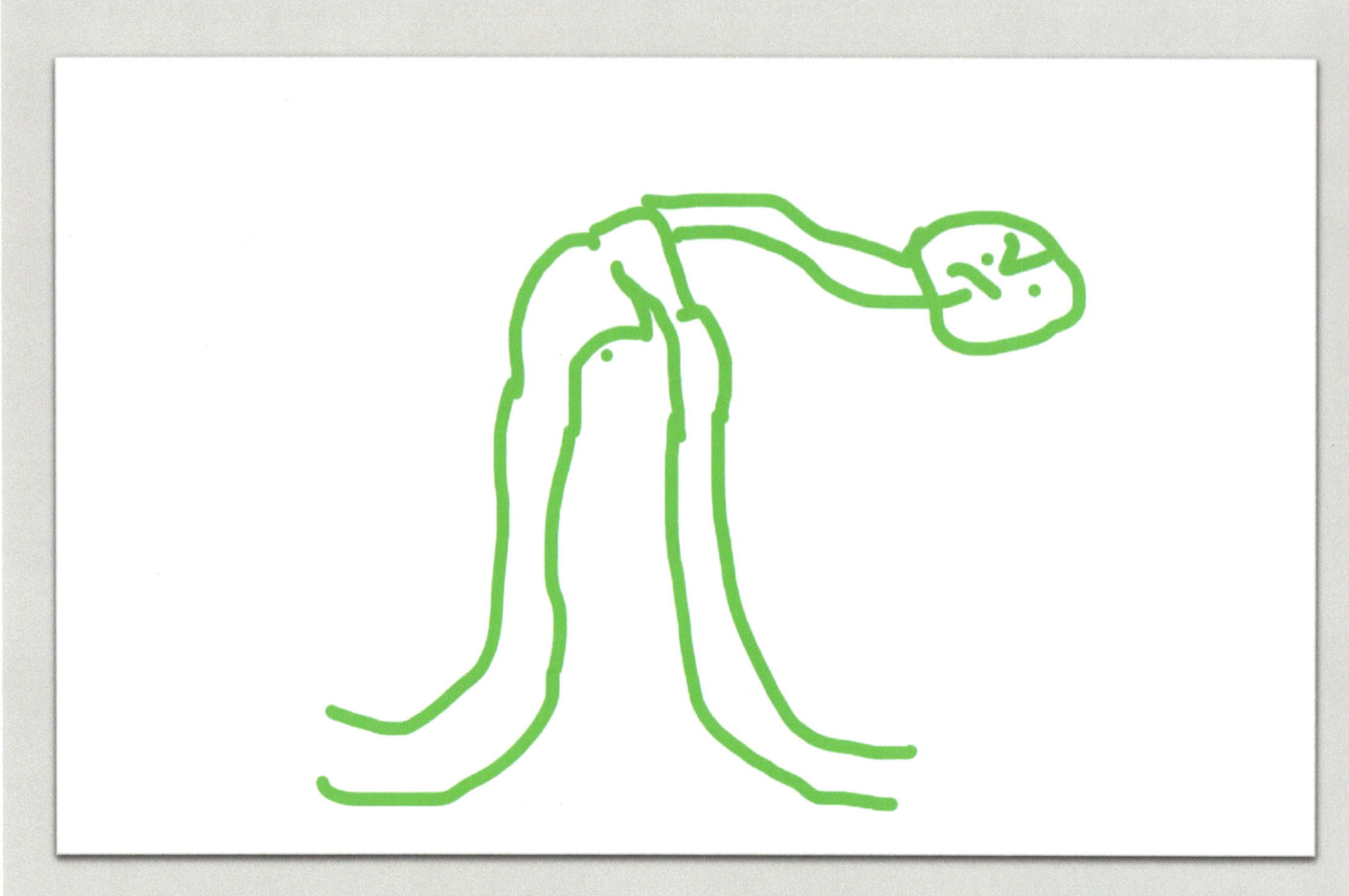

Hengie

This is kengies alter ego the biggest boss in the petz world his claws are mighty sharp with poisonous venom hides under his nails mainly because he hasn't washed his hands in 10 years. Oddly longer than they live.

Petz

"He walks around a silly clown, this petz of mine, oh what a sight!
Although his intentions might be sound, his follies cause us all a fright!"

"A never-ending stream of tricks, while laughter echoes in the air
That's how I'd describe, my petz that's sick, and how he's made me, beware!"

"So much chaos and a sight to see, this petz of mine causes a stir
With never-ending energy, life can't be dull when he's around for sure!"

"Excitement is the only plan when you get a petz that's so peculiar
Like a box of chocolates, you simply can't predict the chaos from our slimy little meddler!"

"A rule-breaking dickhead who just wouldn't quit, and an attitude that won't succumb
No ordinary pet, that I will admit, and so we can always count on some fun!"

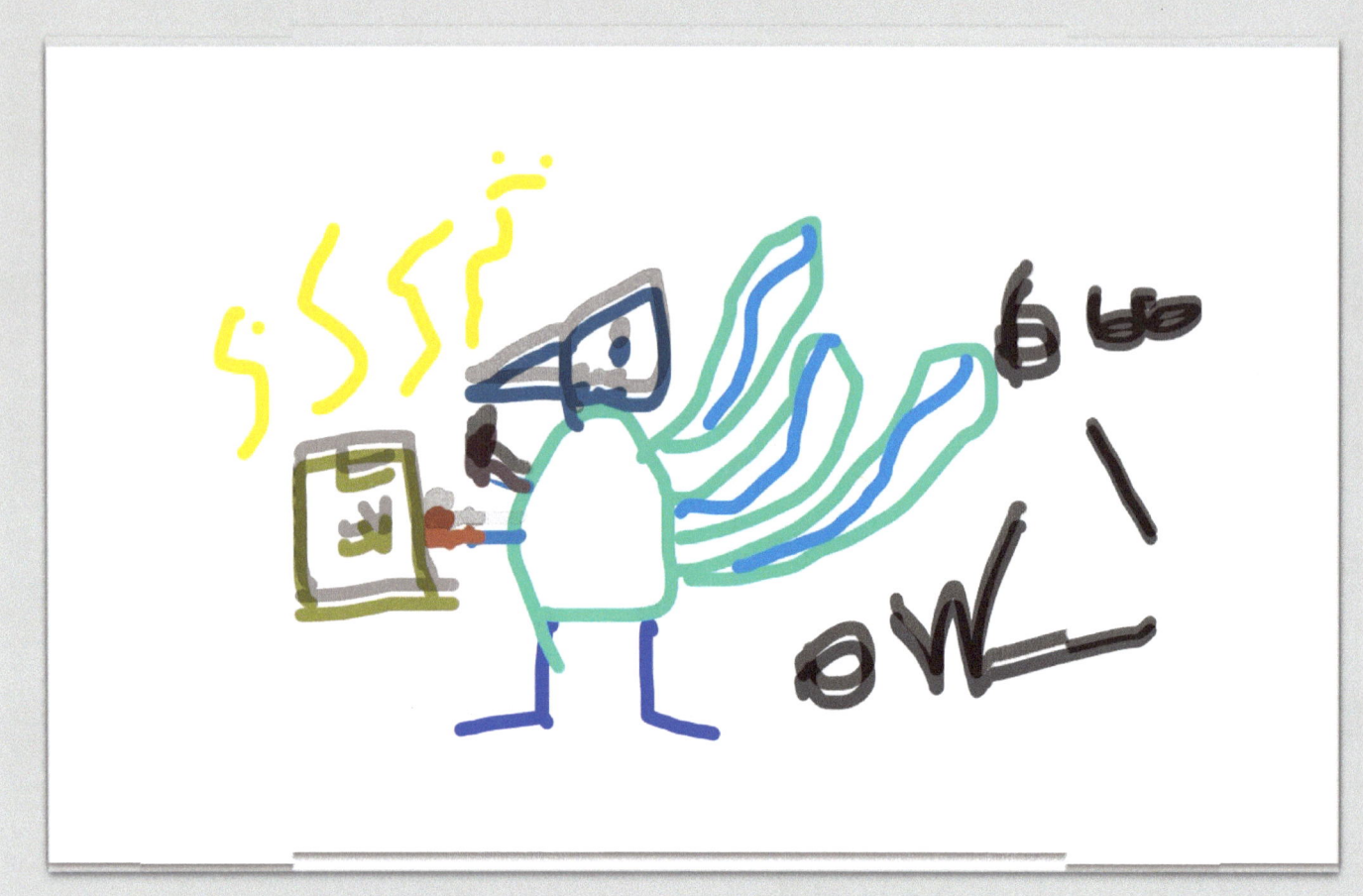

Mikeypeacocky

This petz likes to dance after he failed as a musician. He likes to put on a show to attract the other petz. They are not very good at it and all they attract are greenieflies. Which get stuck in their big bushy tails suffocating and slowly dying while this pet is vainly busy peacocking.

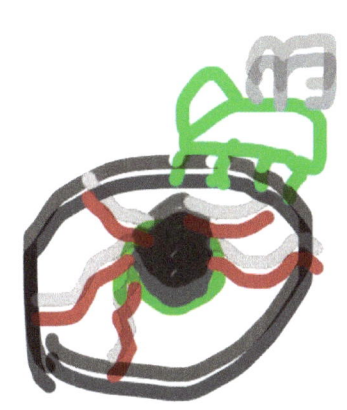

Greenieflies

These pets don't fly despite their confusing name. The legs are actually springs that allows them to hop directly in to either a humans mouth or eyeball for no reason what so ever. The wings are so useless and small no one knows why they have them but we think it's a fashion statement.

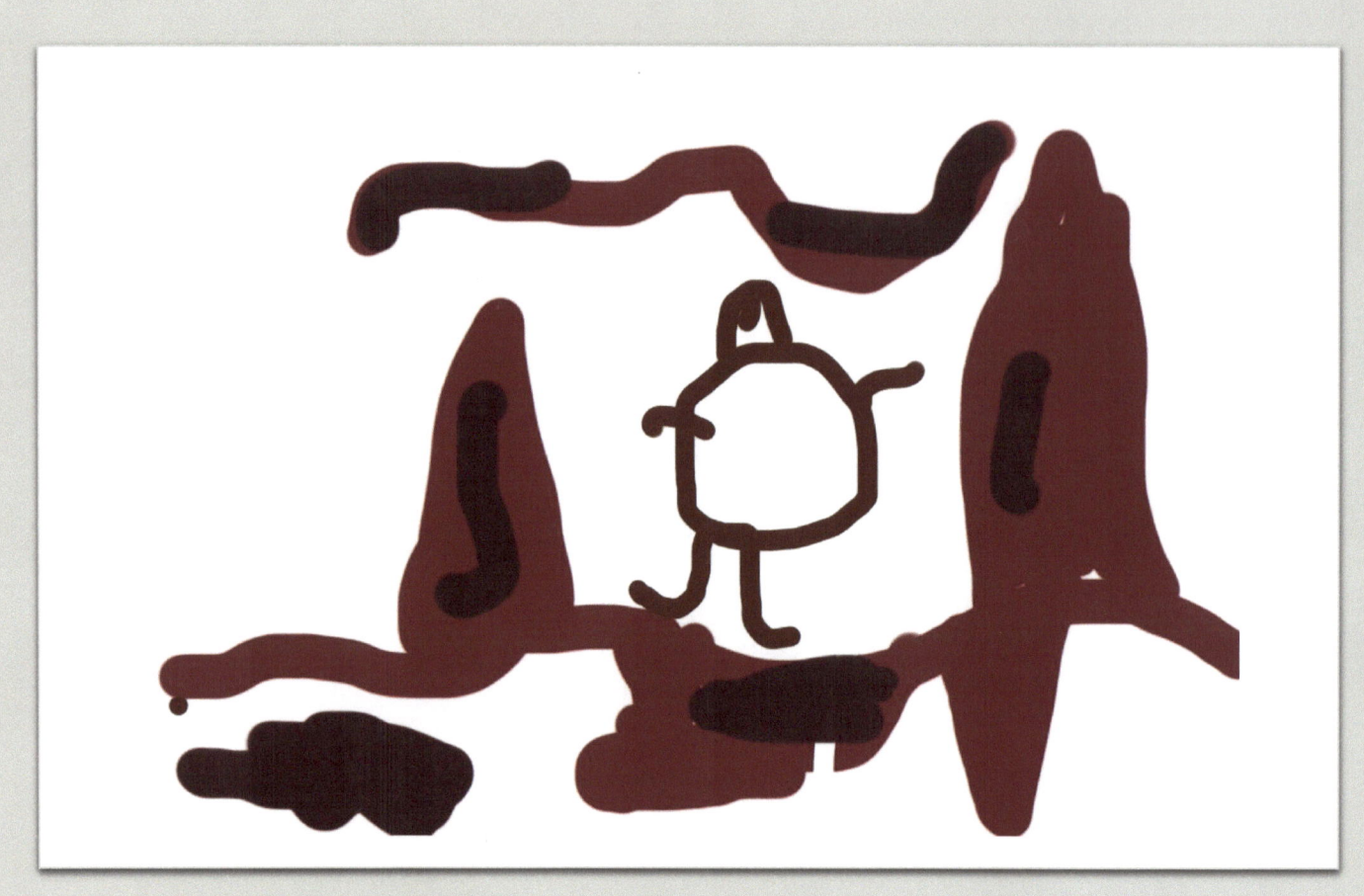

Teddius

This pet has a very round and hairy tummy. Some think he is mean and rude he is not he just has an ugly looking face and a horribly grumpy voice. But no one can see past his exterior to know how loveable he is.

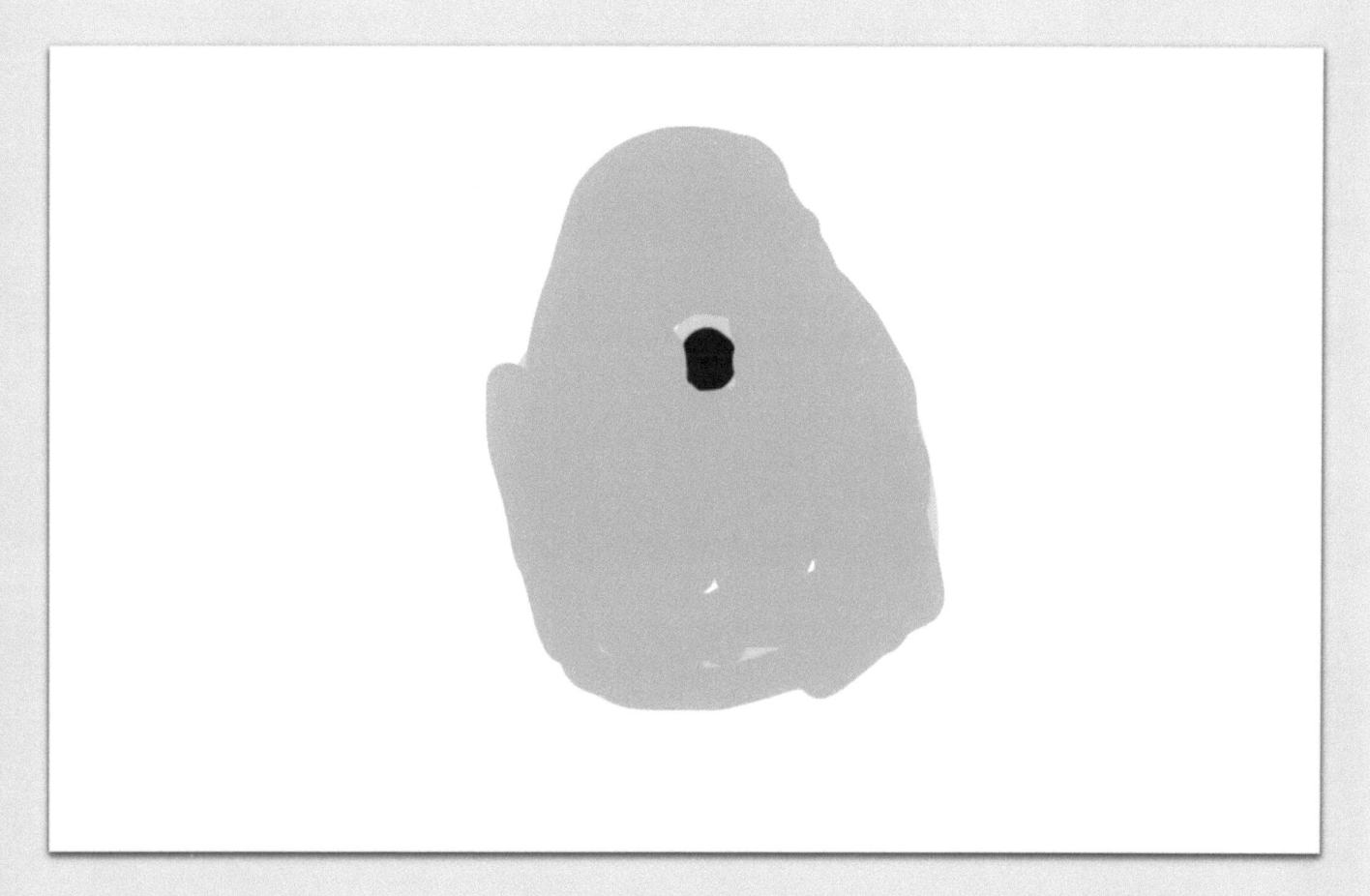

Modo

This petz is a chef he works behind the scenes and if they leave the kitchen they get anxious and crack themselves like an egg. Despite the common myth that eggs can be put back together again this is not true. The Modo dies sunny side up drowning in their own yolk.

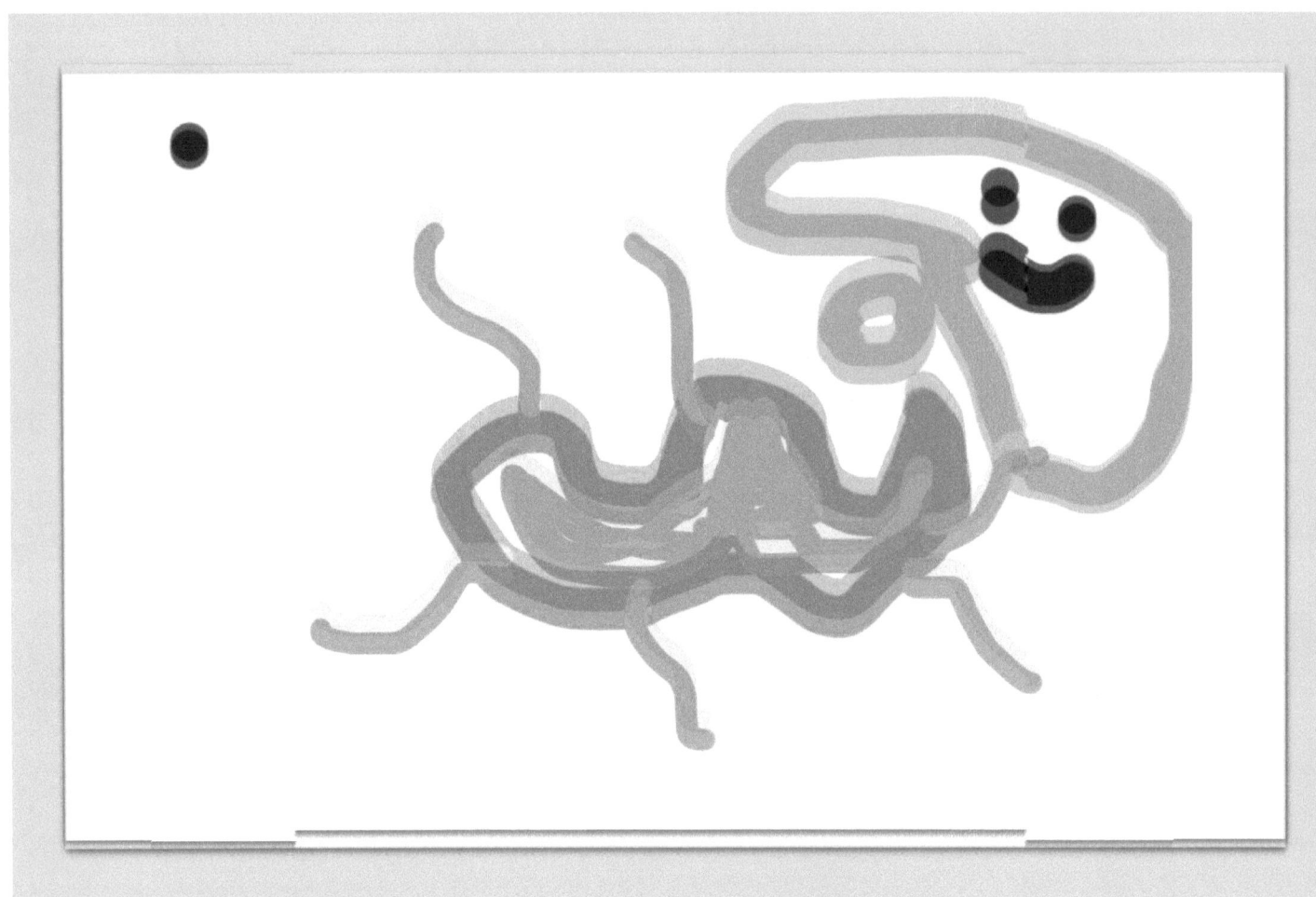

Tattiana

This pet is the most beautiful pet who is also not normal she dreams to be normal but she never will be because she is clearly made completely wrong.

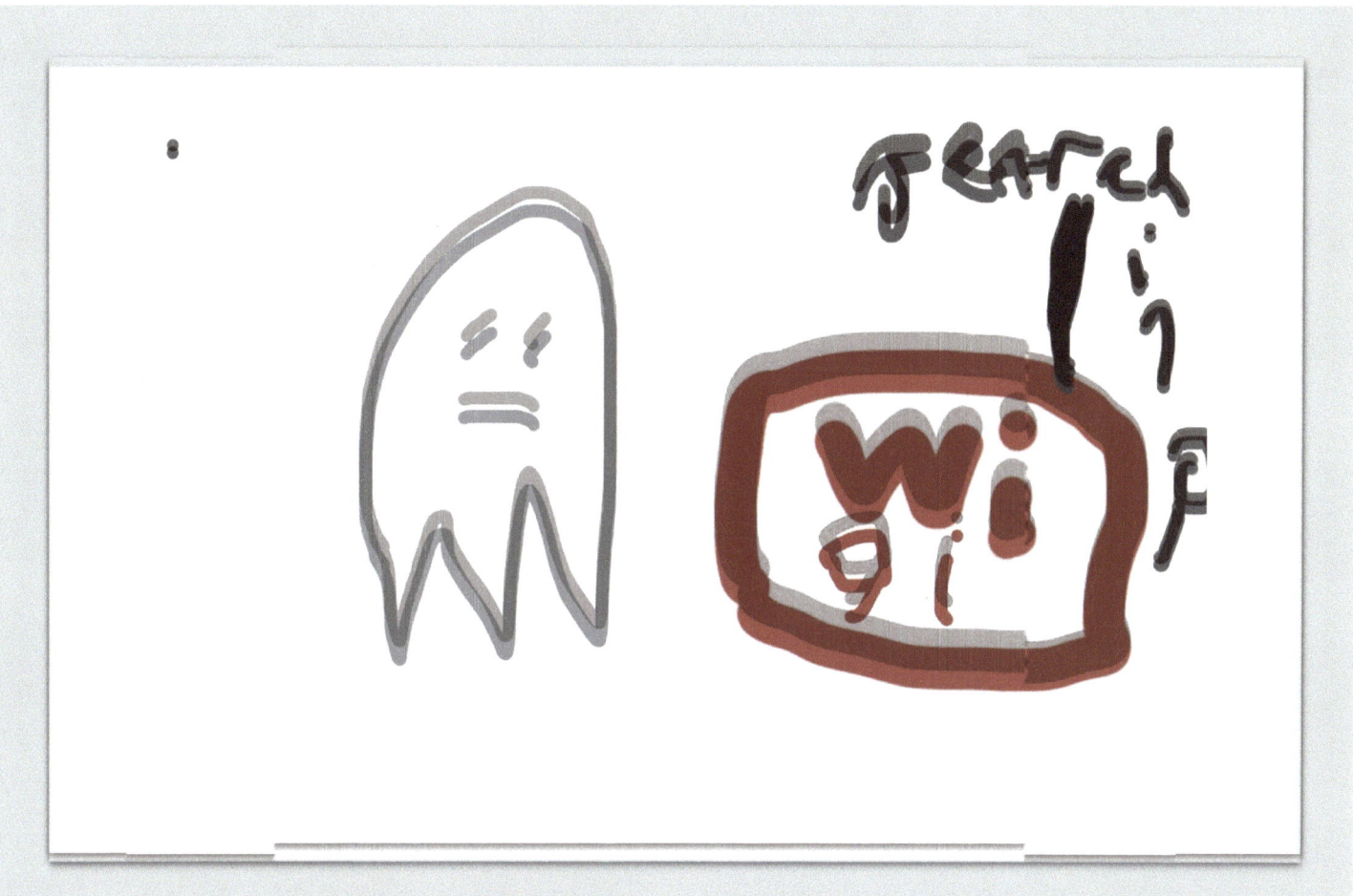

Poshohaz

This pet has a ghostwriter who they can't contact because the WiFi has gone down. We are awaiting his personal statement. Weirdly he looks like a phantom himself and is believed to be his own ghostwriter. Smart isn't it. No it is not.

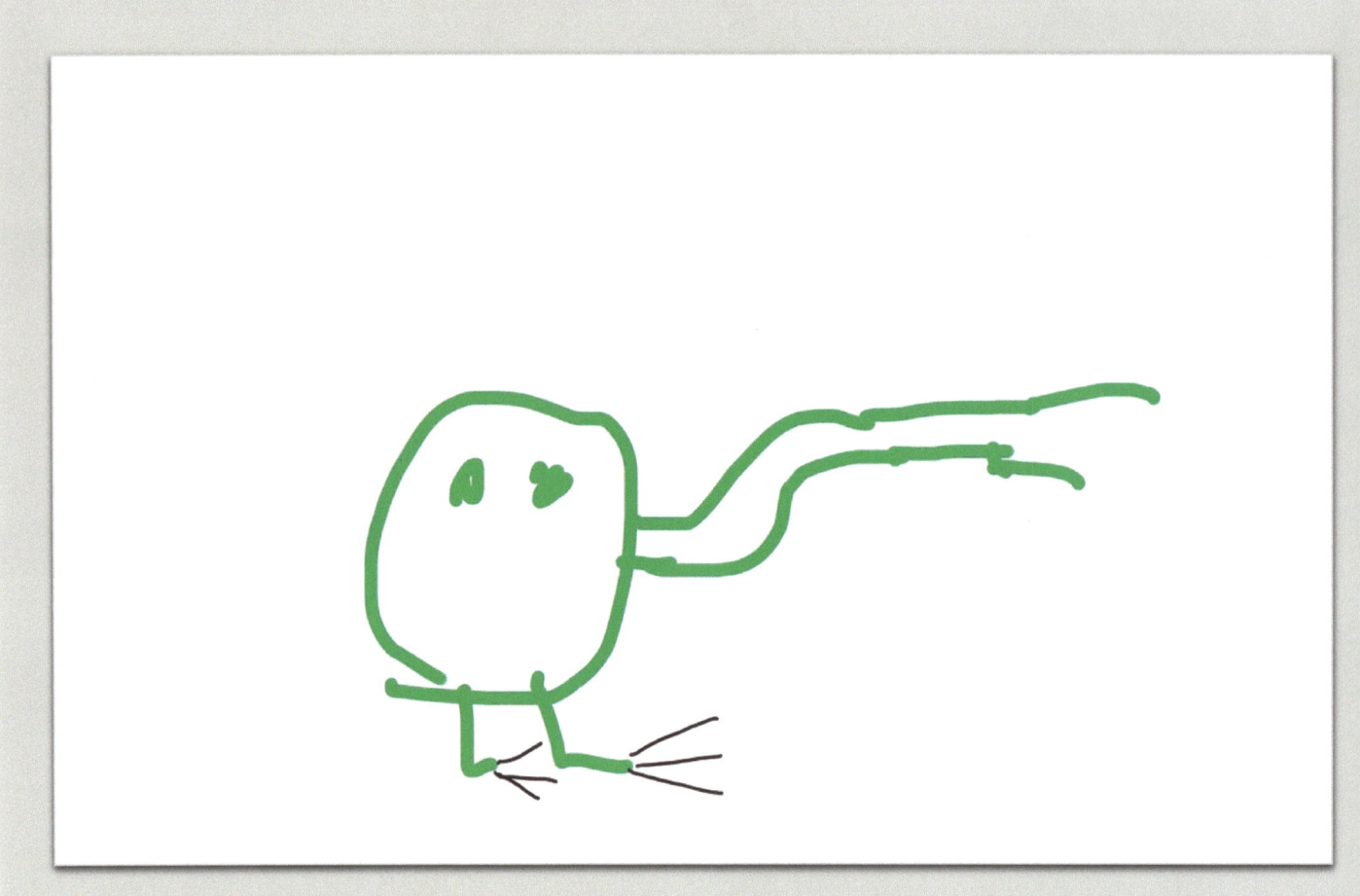

Nurseyblob

This petz is a super spreader. They have long snouts so they can cough directly into your eyeball from 2 meters away. They do t have arms to cover their mouths and wipe the glutenous drool of their own snouts.

Stupid petz
This petz won't scratch its claws when it ought
It's the dumbest pet in the gang, no doubt
Scampering around, no common sense at all
Gets into trouble and thinks it's a ball
He's a silly old pet and he ain't no saint
Going around chasing birds and sniffing paint
Pouncing on bunnies, not learning his lesson
His head's in the clouds, and our hearts are a messin'
That frisky bald petz he's no fool
Making funny sounds that nearly sound cool
And if looking at it were allowed
You'd wonder how on earth it is so proud
I'm playing with the petz that can't listen
Fur flying about, it's quite the vision
Opportunities for entertainment come by and stay
And these pets have no idea what I'm trying to say
This is a word of advice and one that's worth knowing
When it comes to this petz, it's best left flowing
The likeliest outcome is a great annoyance
If not handled with care, there is absolutely no point

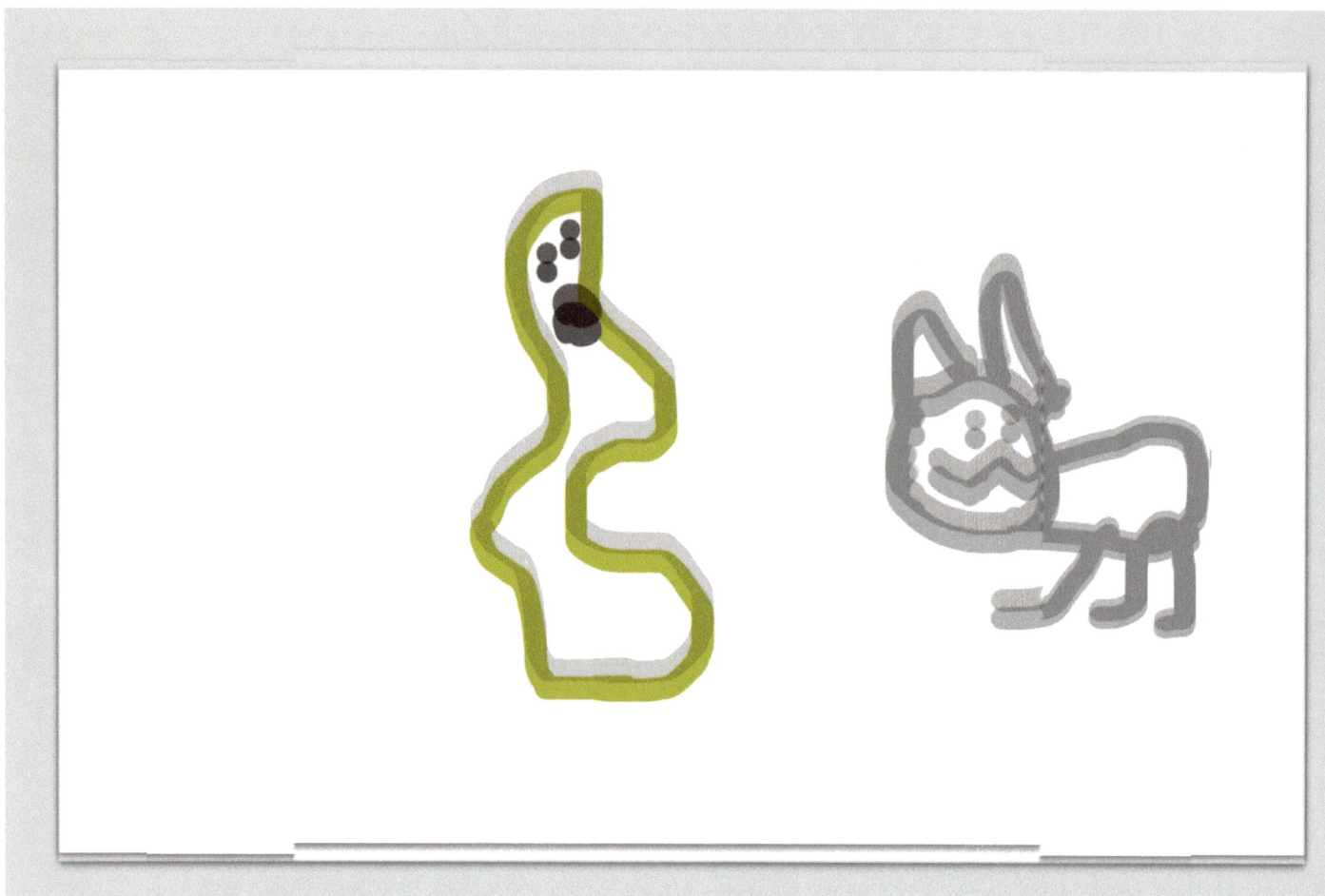

Nomnom

This pet eats so many noodles they devolve in to a noodle and get eaten by kittis

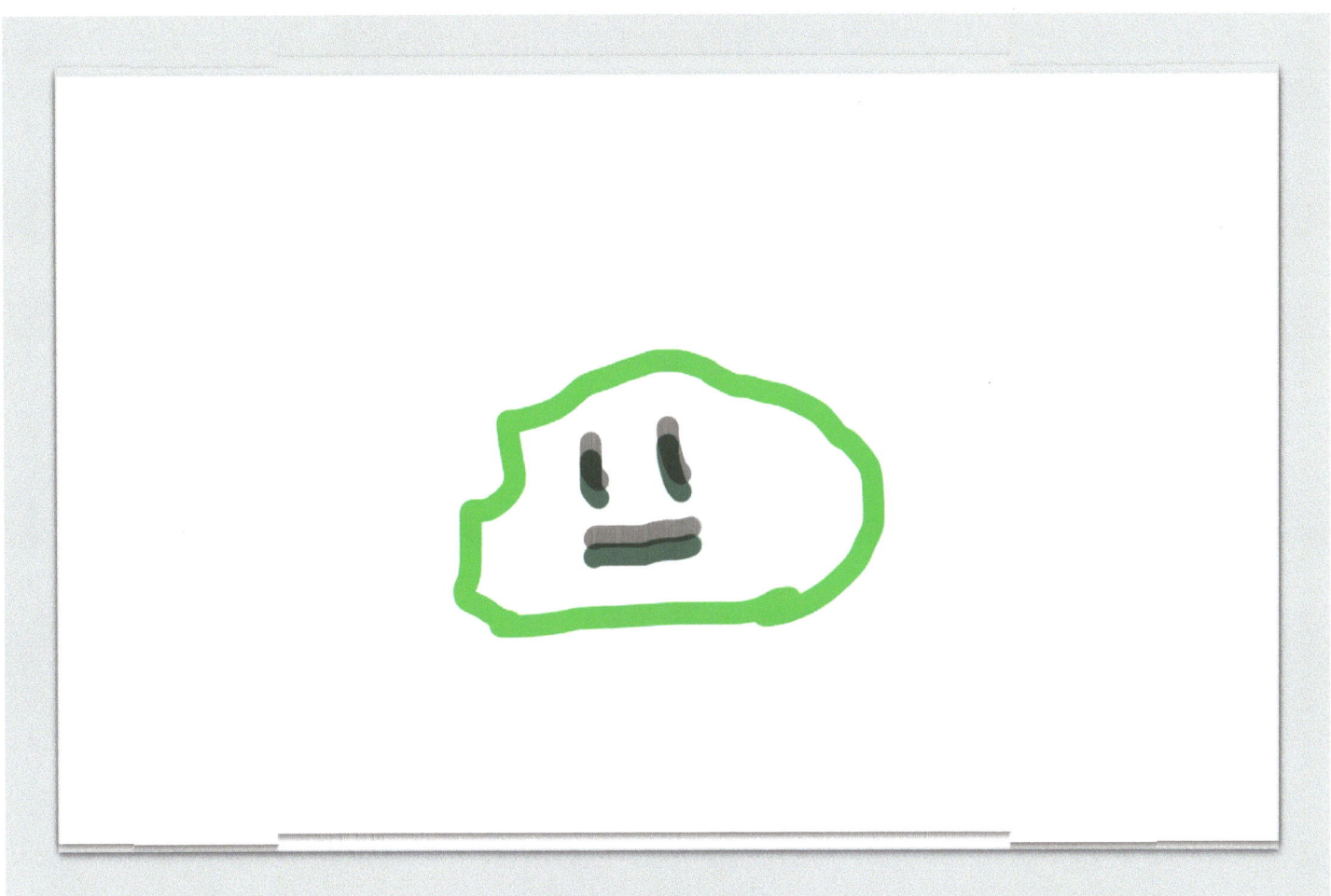

Bleb

Catches prey by sticking to their faces and suffocating them it's suckers are impossible to prize off unfortunately it can't catch anything as I can't move from the rock it was born on.

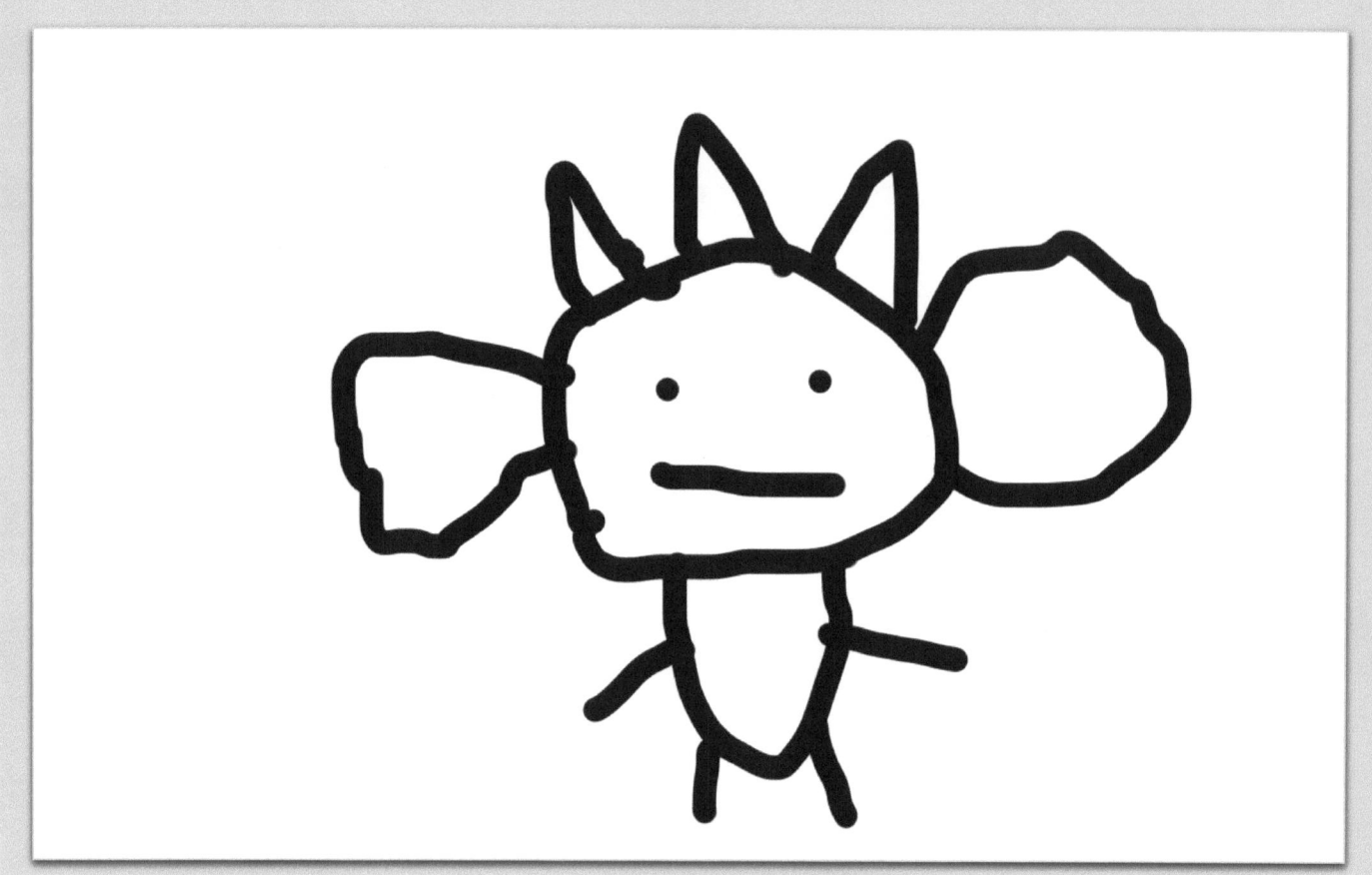

Elmopea

Rushes through the house and dies by bumping into a elmopeaguzler

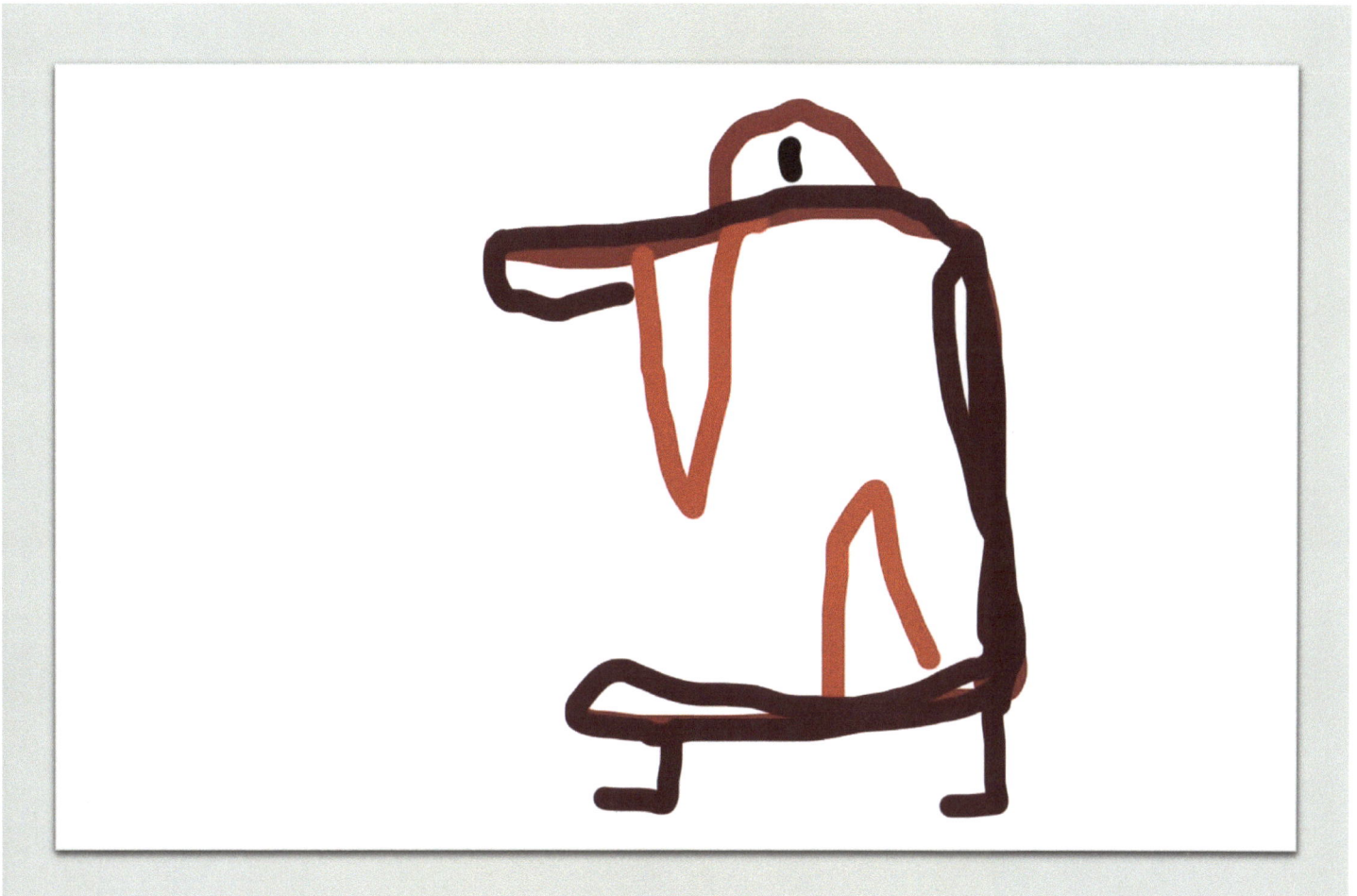

Elmopeaguzzler

They eat elmopeas but they are terrified of adult hengies.

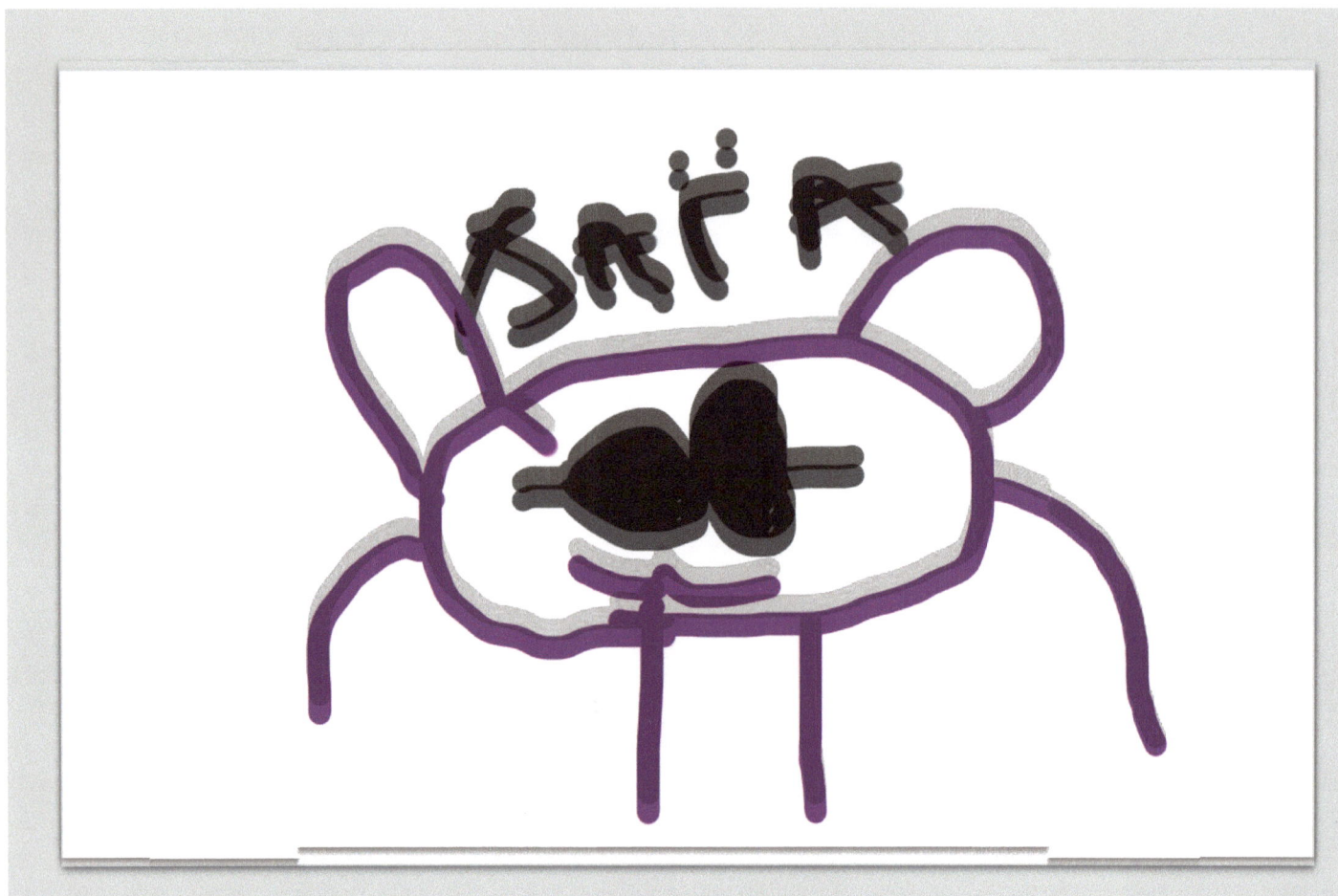

Sarä

The dots on this petz name are pointless but they put them on to pretend to be cooler than other petz. They actually are cooler because they have two dots in their name.

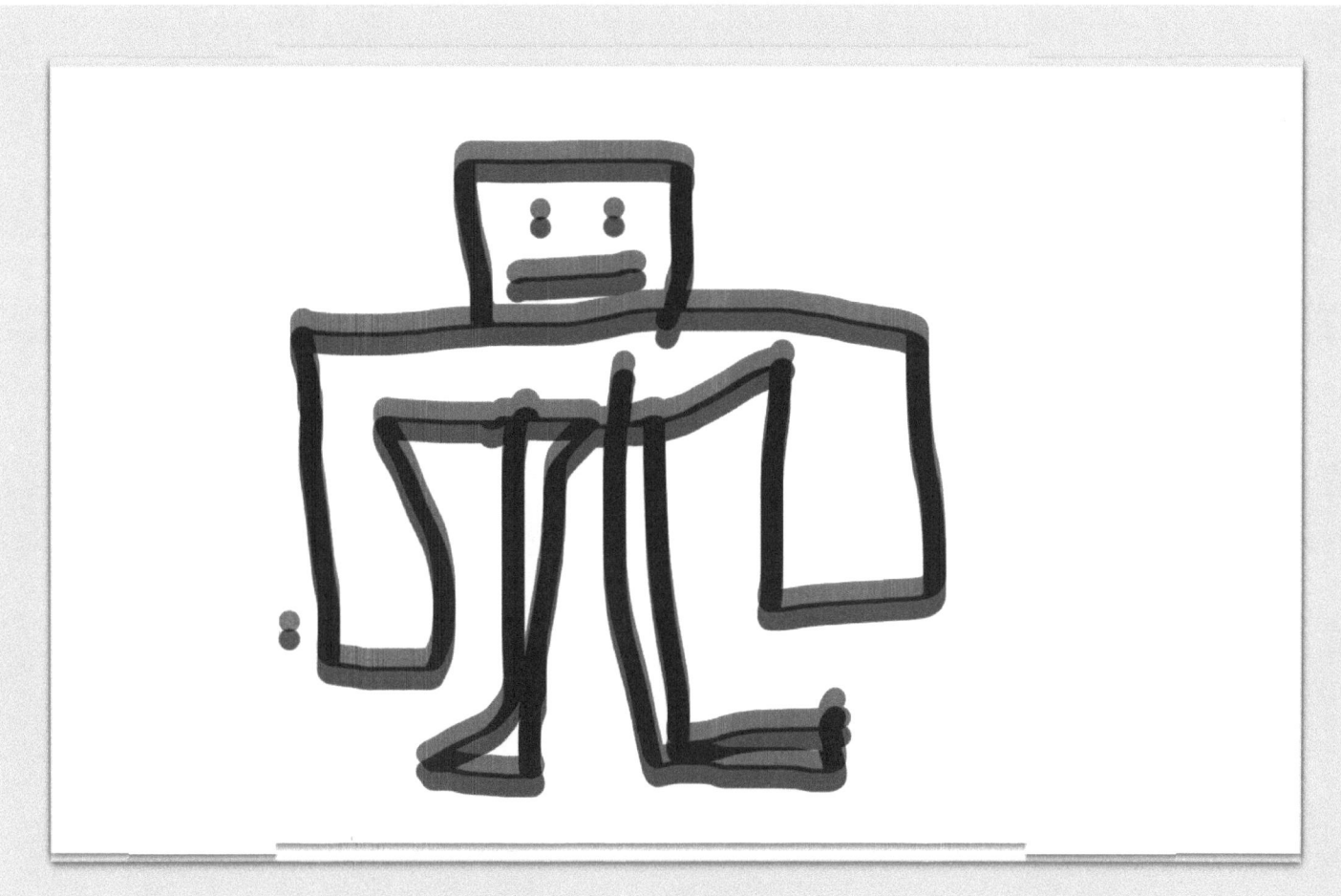

Winger
It does nothing then dies.

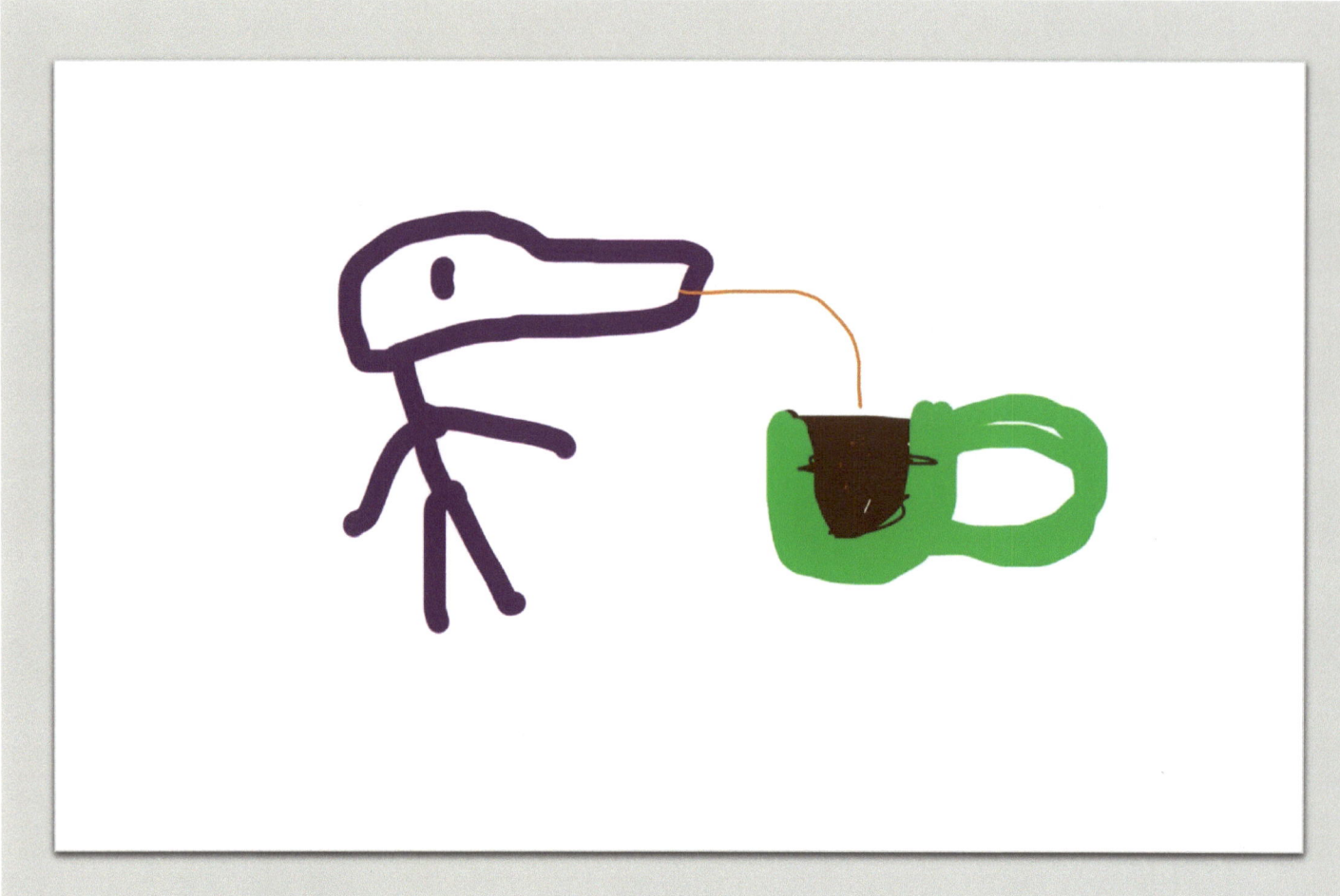

Scrotopia

Drinks a lot of Yorkshire tea then dies

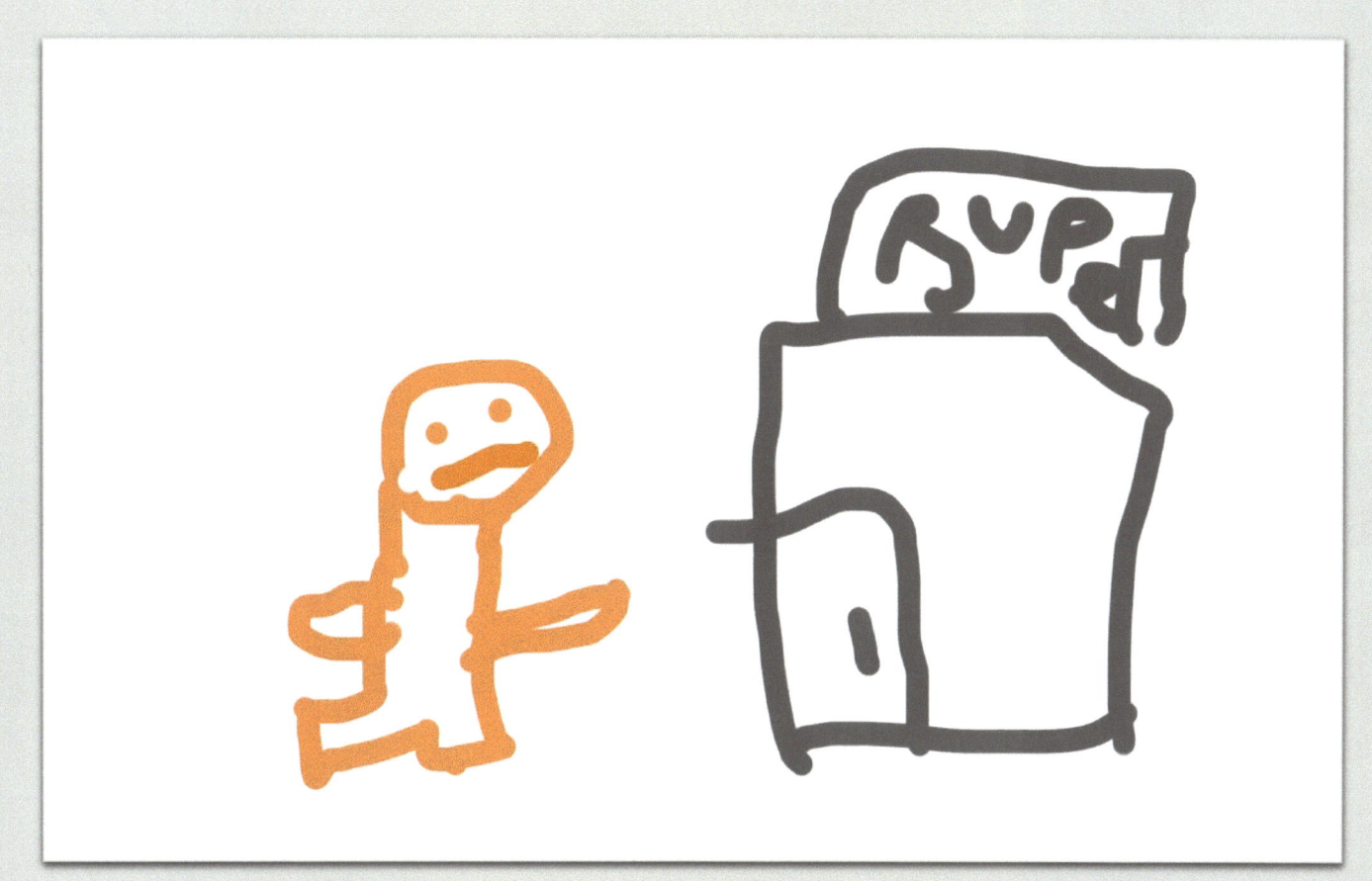

Flange

Flanges never stops running and going to the supermarket. They are worried of running out of food and have hoards at home, way more than they need. They are selfish and like to make sure that if something went wrong in the world that they would be the last one to survive because that sounds really great doesn't it. Being alive all on your own.

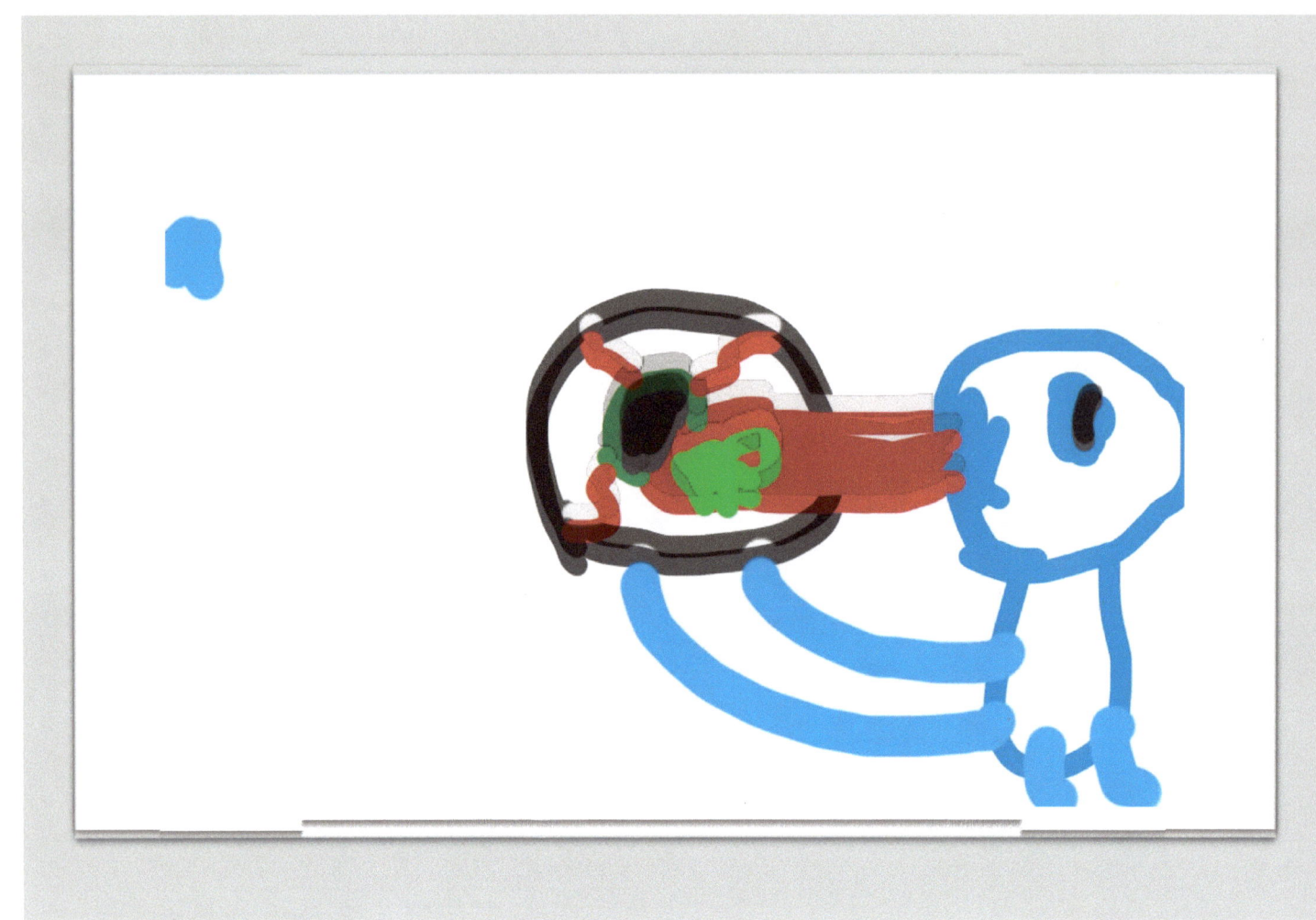

Cystoad
He licks dead greenflies out of human eyes

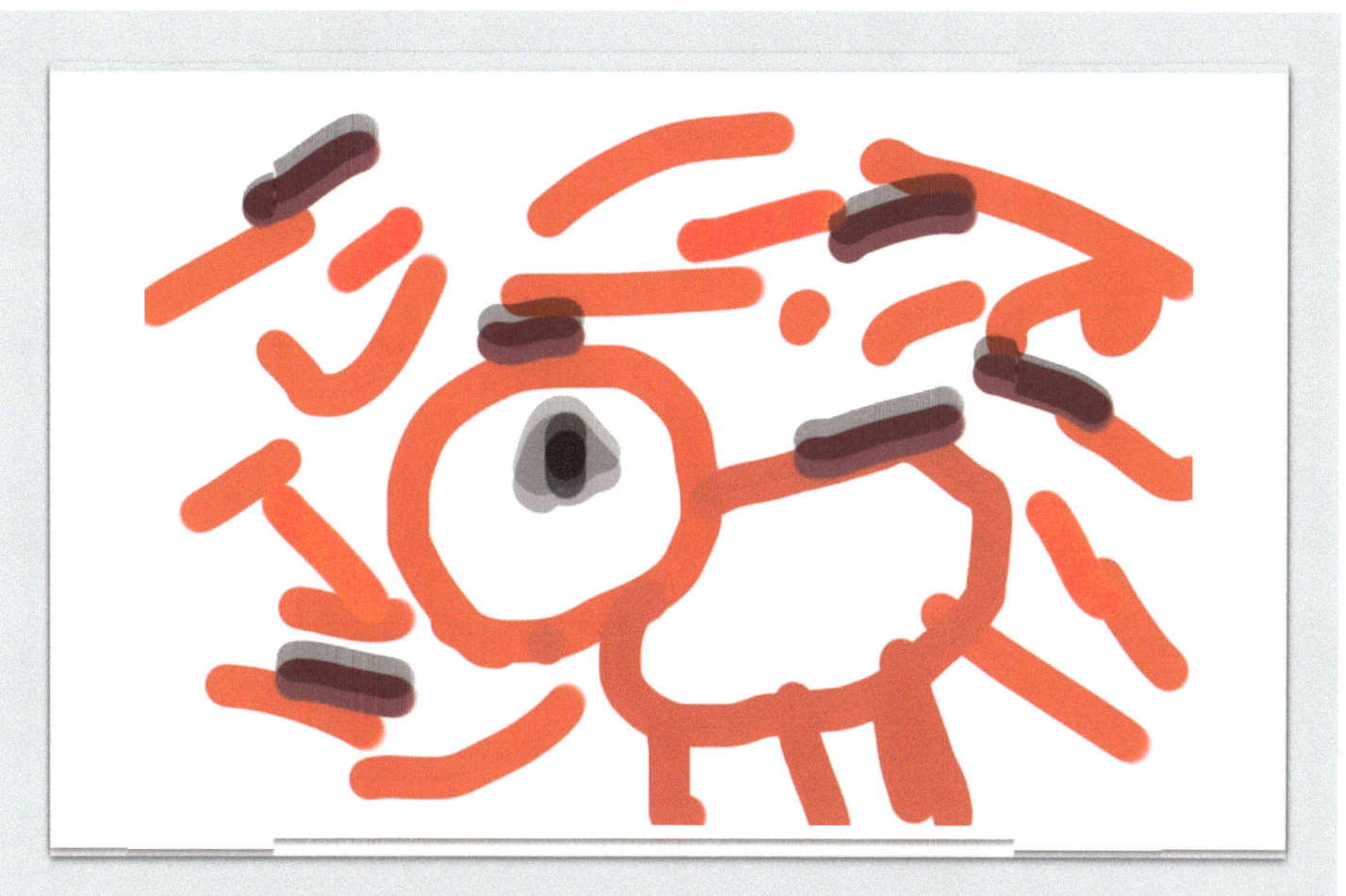

Ovariangst

Self destructs at any given opportunity. But is needed to be cruelly kept alive for the survival of all petz species. This petz has been medically neglected its entire existence even though it is what reproduces every petz species. It feels gloppy and sulks milky tears that others harvest and drink for strength.

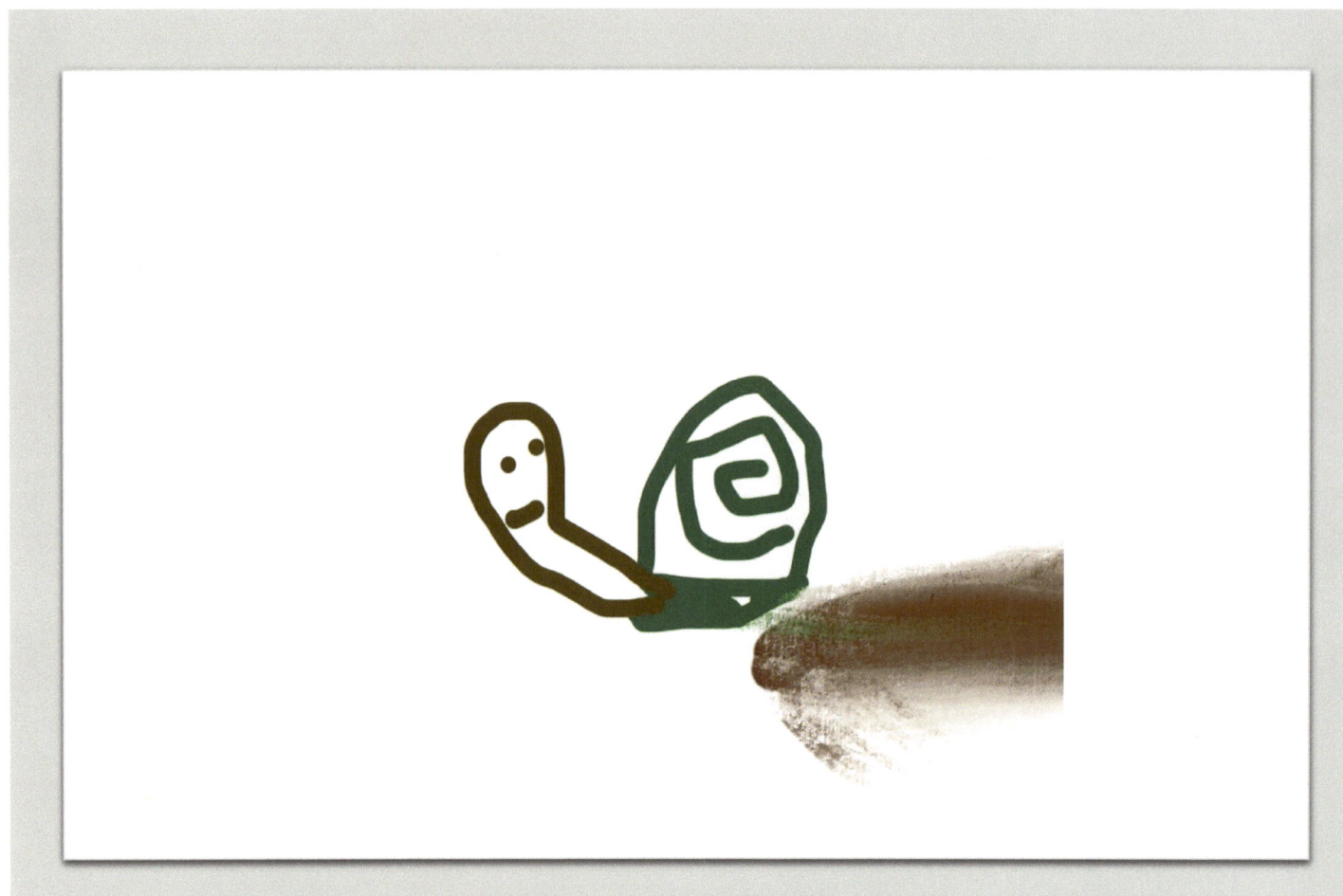

Skidrick

He leaves his sticking trail all over the place and then dies after running out of bottom flap juice.

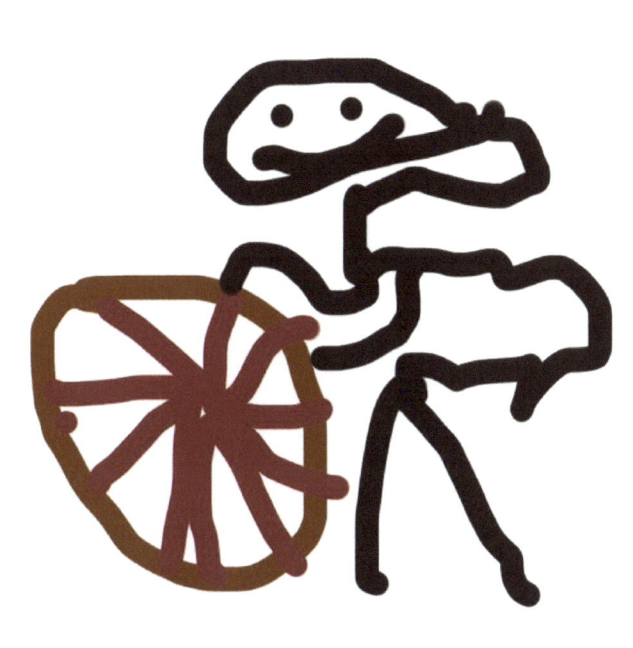

Kieth

He only eats quiche and he is very boring there isn't much to say about him infact he is so boring he's actually halarious if you think about him too long. Don't do that it's a waste of time he adds and contributes nothing to the petz world.

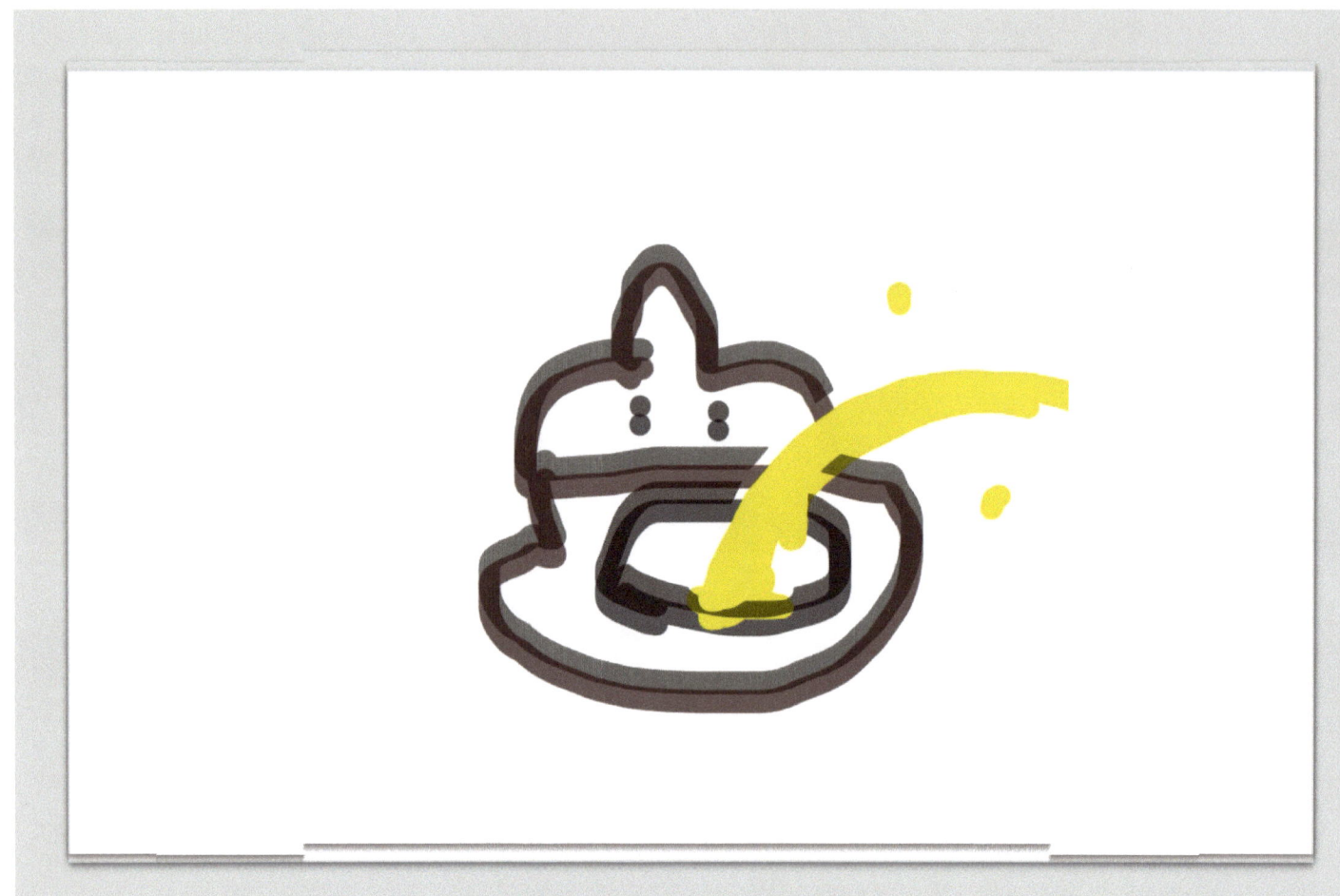

Kieth's poo

Although Kieth's are useless they reproduce Mutatated quiche fectalal matter. its inner clumpcorns become incredibly violent for no reason and attack hengies with putrid acidic wee.

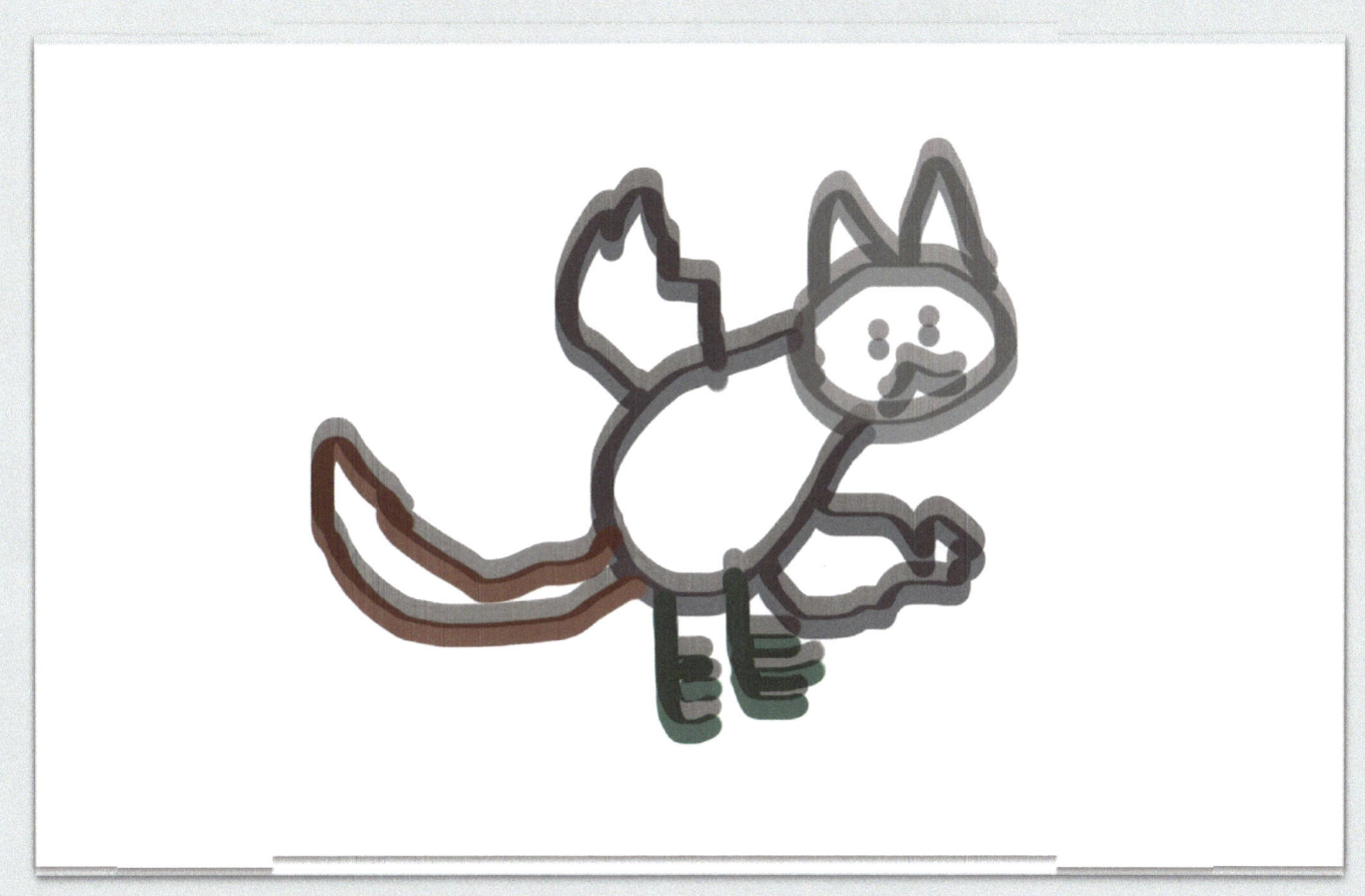

Mashamal

is like a kinda Greek mythology animal with lots of different personalities and body parts stolen of others and glued together. what they do apart from take selfies and walk around looking incredibly cool and beautiful is a mystery. They are never happy.

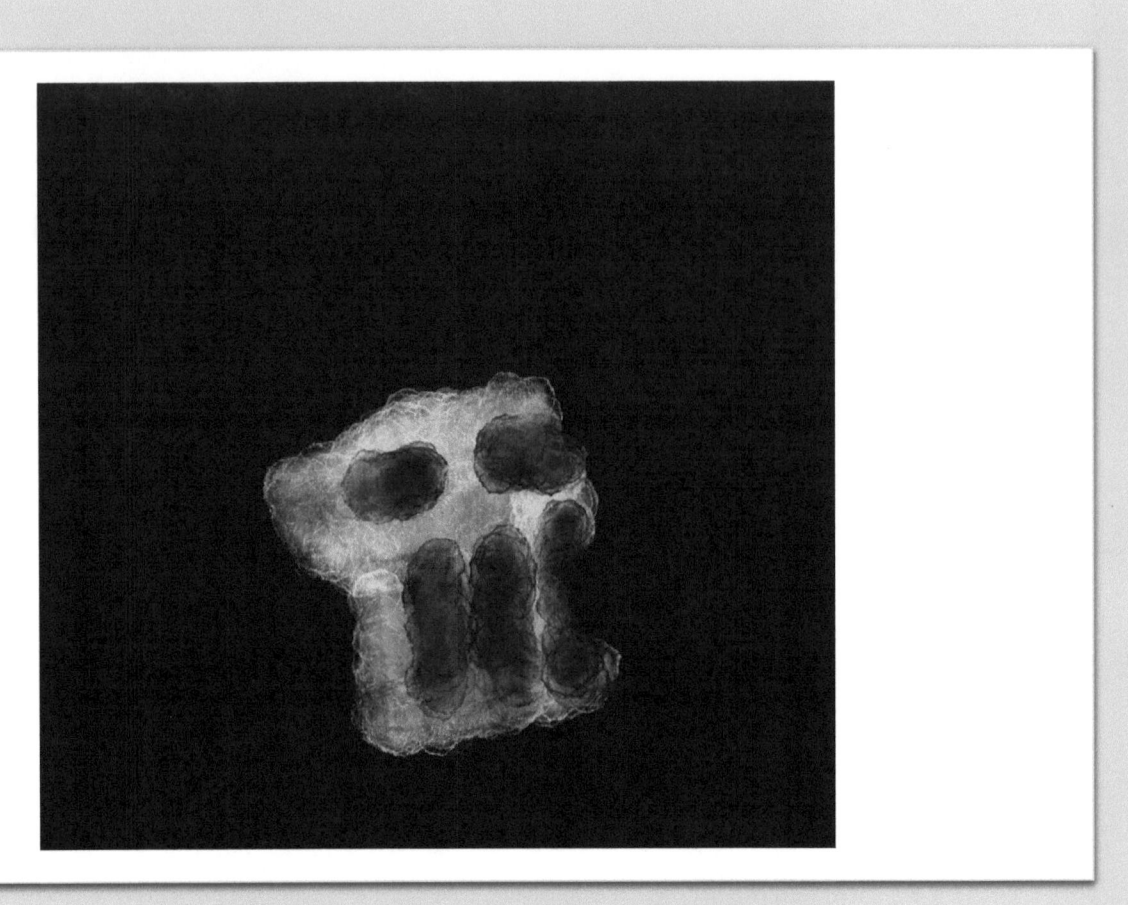

Blehluhgeddonechined

A really boring petz and the same as a winger. They sit around waiting for death the only thing that keeps them going is the pain of not being dead yet.

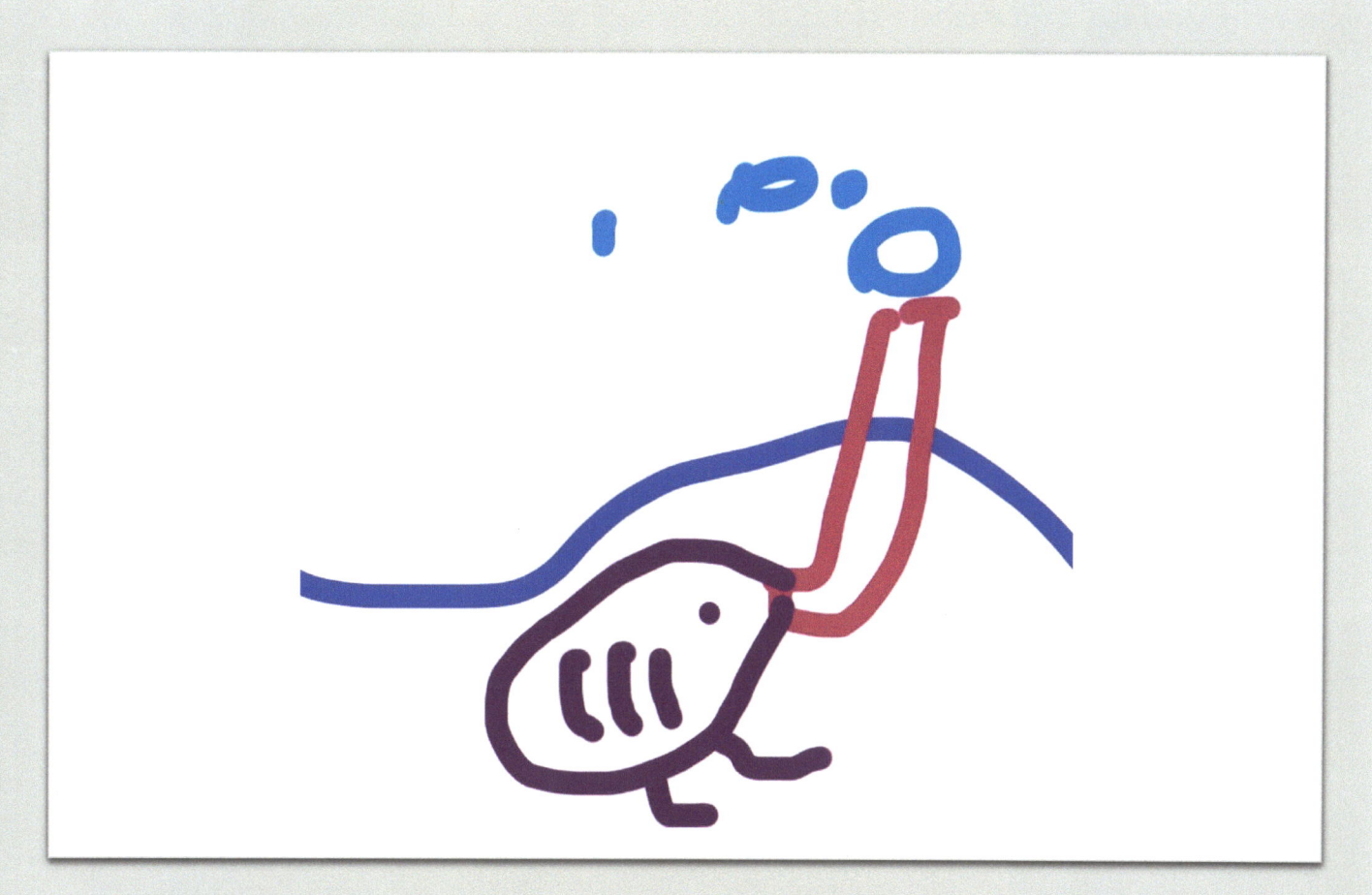

Snorkl

The stay high up in the sea where there is little fish to eat. when they start to starve they dive down to get food but they ultimately drown because they haven't properly mutated to survive in the sea without a plastic snorkel they find at birth in the ocean floor and become dependent on it.

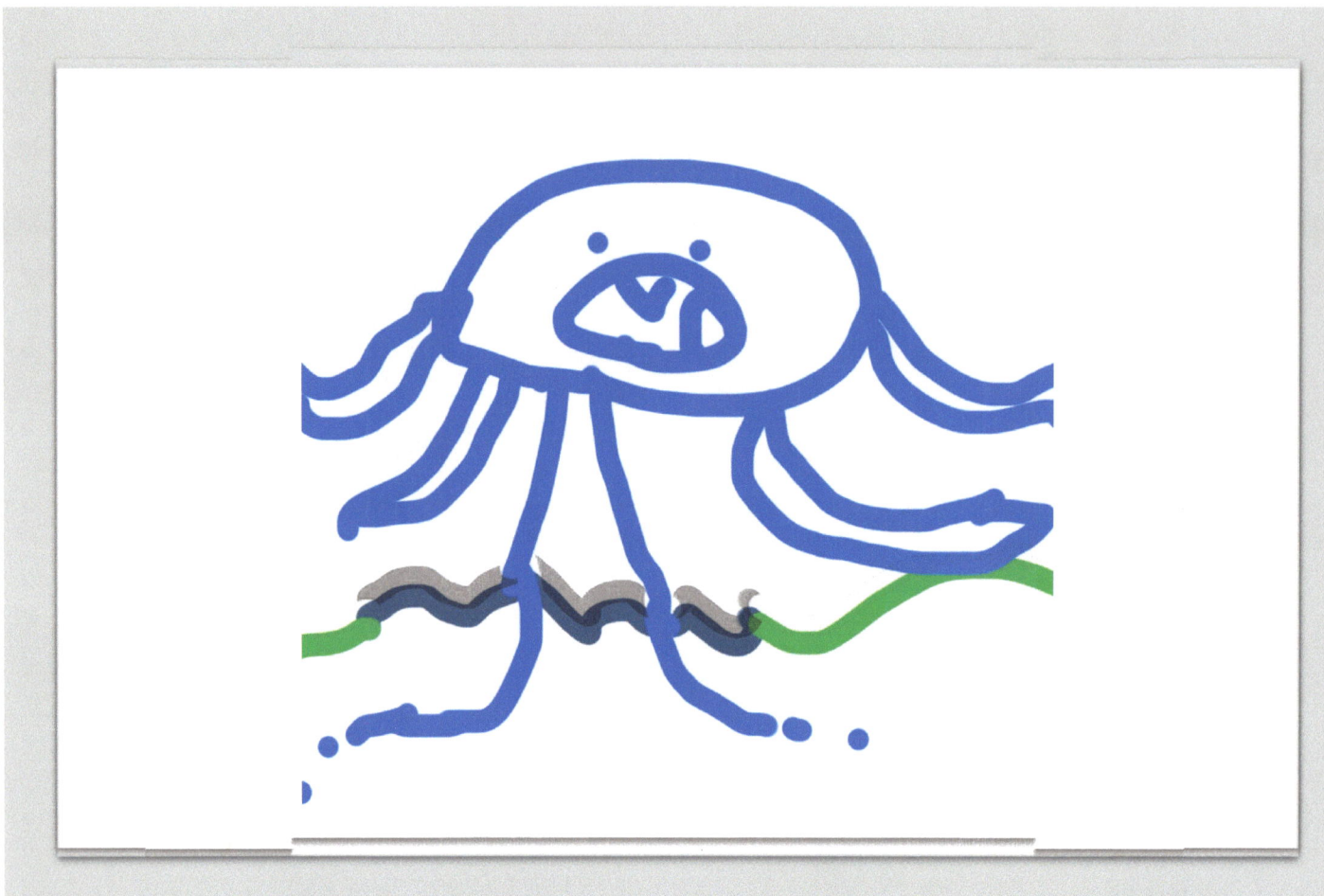

Adult snorkl

If they manage to survive they will go to land make a puddle and call it home. When they get older they grow legs and kill anything in their path. Don't worry not all adult snorkels are like that. Just joking some are worse.

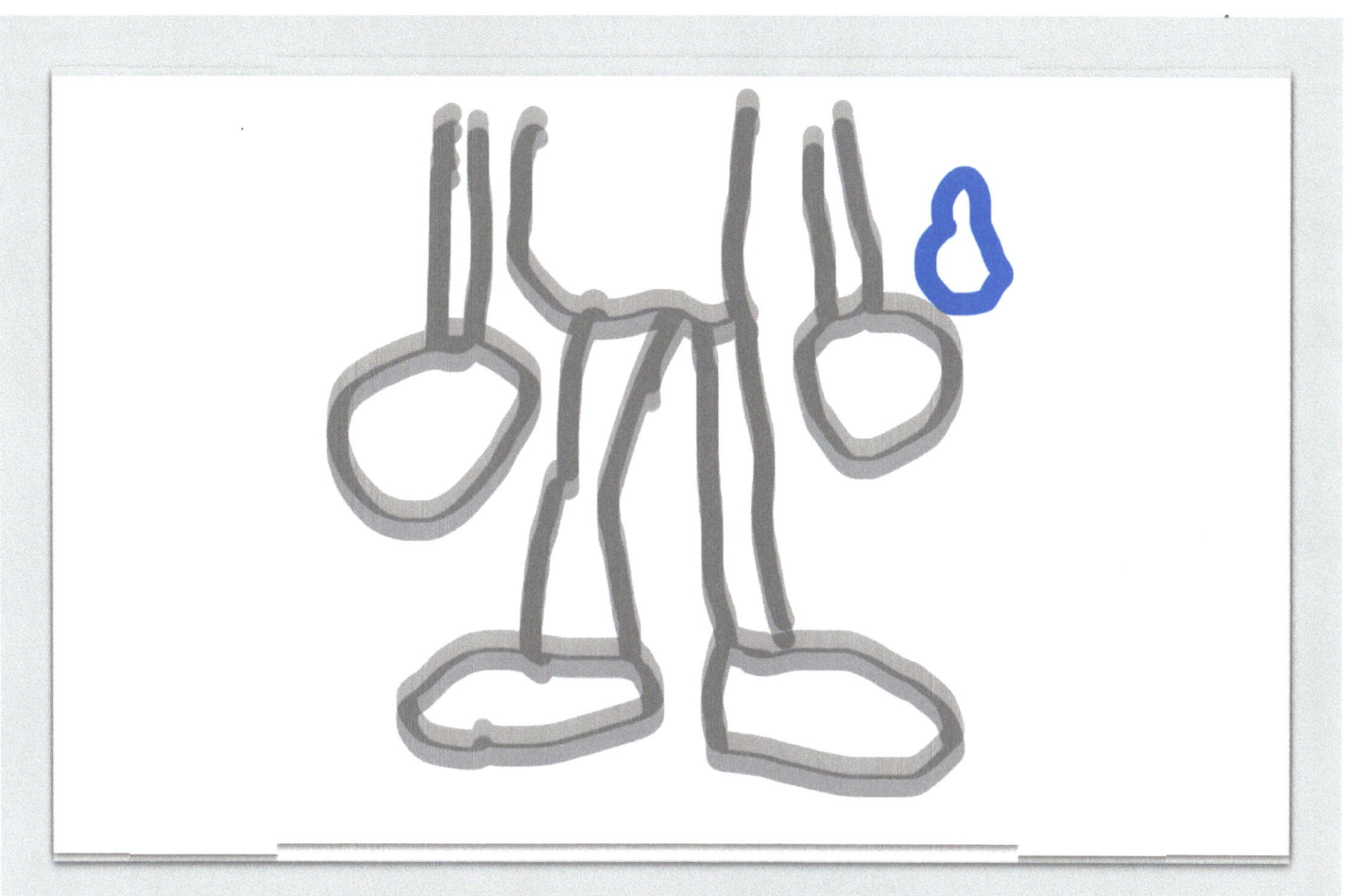

Lev

Lev falls in love with Blebs so they chase after the Blebs to propose but blebs can't moves so they get stomped on by the levs and then levs cry to death

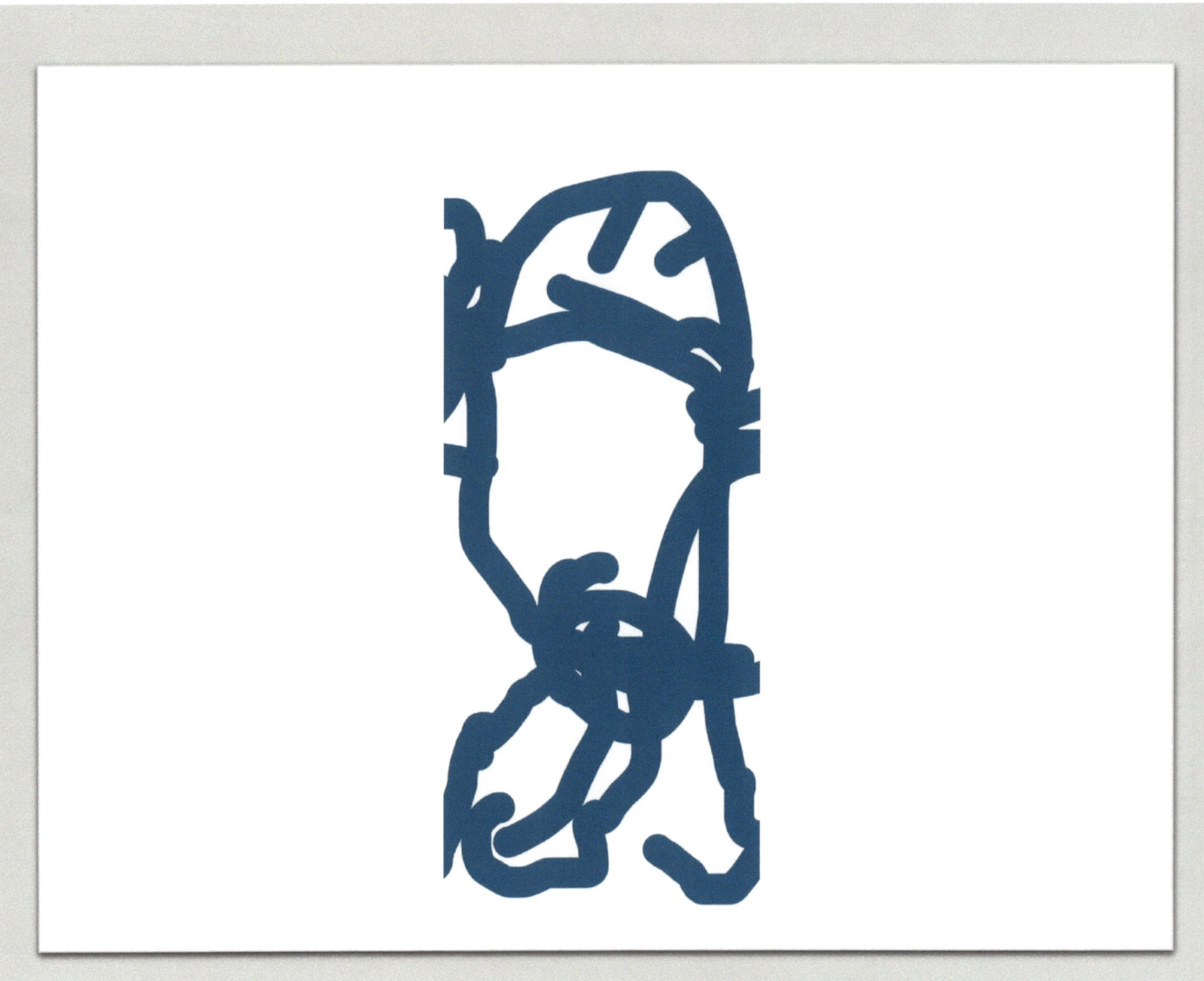

He's not meant to be here

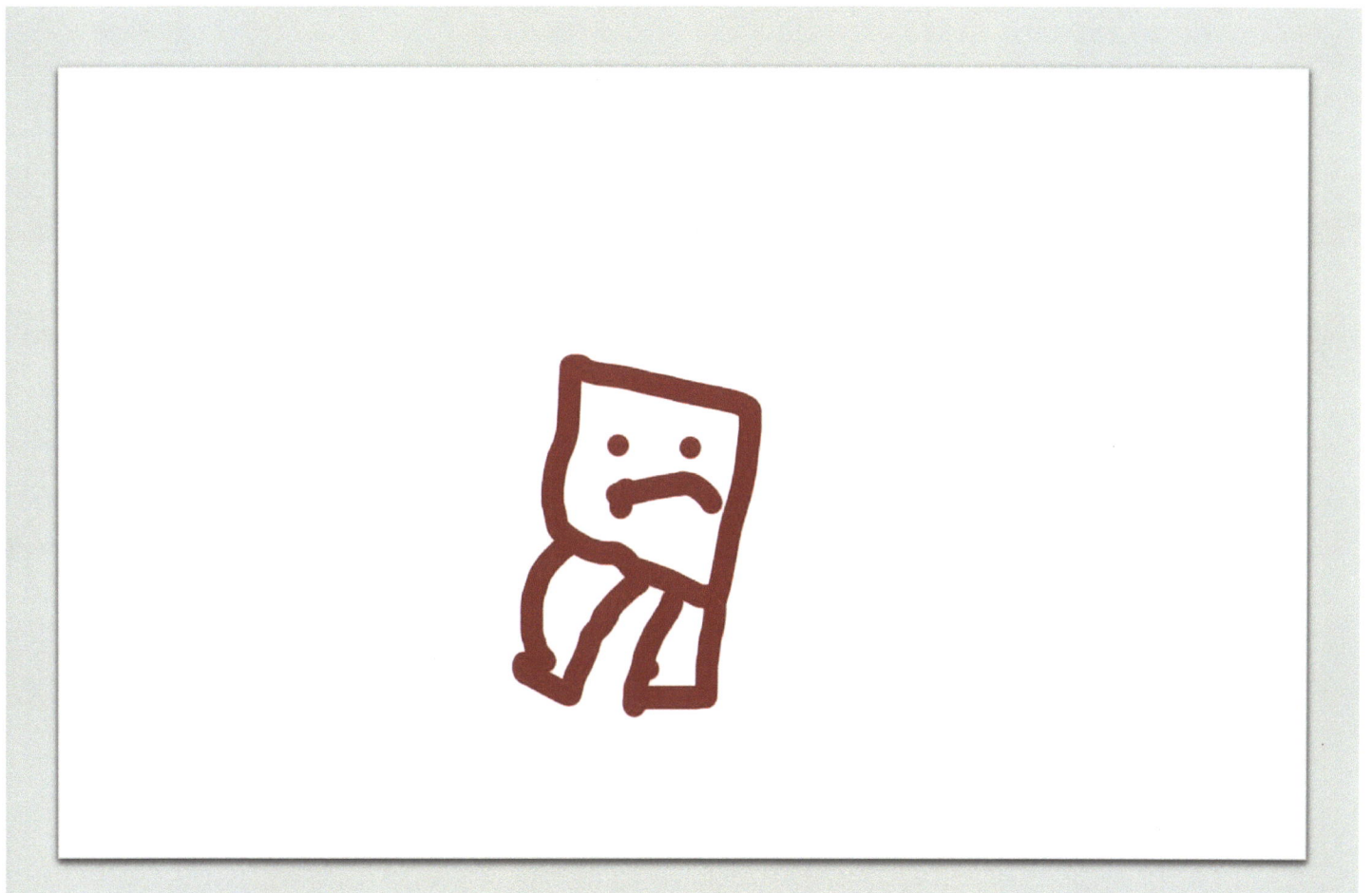

Cube
spends his existence jumping on sofas. Until it falls off and breaks its skull, forming it into an advanced species of Petz